2 A.M.

Other Writings by Walter Lanyon

Abd Allah, Teacher, Healer
And It Was Told of a Certain Potter
Behold the Man ◆ Demonstration
Embers ◆ The Eyes of the Blind
I Came ◆ The Impatient Dawn
Impressions of a Nomad
It Is Wonderful ◆ The Joy Bringer
A Lamp unto My Feet
The Laughter of God ◆ Leaves of the Tree
A Light Set upon a Hill
London Notes and Lectures
Out of the Clouds
Quintology: Ask and Ye Shall Receive
A Royal Diadem
That Ye Might Have
The Temple Not Made with Hands
Thrust in the Sickle ◆ Treatment
Without the Smell of Fire
Your Heritage

Available through:
Mystics of the World
Eliot, Maine
www.mysticsoftheworld.com

2 A.M.

Walter C. Lanyon

2 A.M.

Mystics of the World First Edition 2015
Published by Mystics of the World
ISBN-13: 978-0692396162
ISBN-10: 0692396160

> For information contact:
> Mystics of the World
> Eliot, Maine
> www.mysticsoftheworld.com

Cover graphics by Margra Muirhead
Printed by CreateSpace
Available from Mystics of the World and Amazon.com

ৡ ৶

Walter C. Lanyon, 1887 – 1967
Originally published 1944

Contents

Foreword 9
Chapter I
    Integrity to Instinct... 11
Chapter II
    A Spinner in the Sun 13
Chapter III
    Flying 17
Chapter IV
    Painting a Room Green 23
Chapter V
    The Magic Circle... 25
Chapter VI
    Realm of Manifestation 34
Chapter VII
    Light 39
Chapter VIII
    The God within You 51
Chapter IX
    Increase 54
Chapter X
    In a Dream — In a Vision.................................... 59
Chapter XI
    It Is Consummated 62
Chapter XII
    Let God Let.. 68

Chapter XIII
    They Say 74
Chapter XIV
    Shadows.. 93
Chapter XV
    So You Won't Talk?... 109
Chapter XVI
    From an Old London Note Book 135
Chapter XVII
    Taking Thought 148
Chapter XVIII
    The No-Treatment Man................................... 156
Chapter XIX
    The Dimension of Infinity 166
Chapter XX
    Mary 178
About the Author... 185

*I say no man has ever yet been
half devout enough,
None has ever yet adored
or worship'd half enough,
None has begun to think
how divine he himself is,
and how certain the future is.
I say that the real and permanent
grandeur of these States
must be their religion,
Otherwise there is no real
and permanent grandeur.*
—Walt Whitman

Foreword

This book was written, for the most part, at 2 A.M.—that is the *why* of the name. Awakened at that hour nearly every night for more than a year, great bursts of light and revelation came through, and so I jotted them down. I thought you might like to browse through them—so many of them have proved workable.

Here they are. Only one page in the entire manuscript had to be partially rewritten; the rest of the book is exactly as it came through except, of course, for punctuation and spelling. I never could spell very well—how about you? Do you have any difficulty making words sort of grotesque? Do you sometimes throw in an occasional mute "e"?

I make all sorts of excuses for myself, as you may do too. Once I had to spell in three languages; and of course, there is always solace in the fact that several great men couldn't spell. Well, who started this argument about spelling? If a governess, a couple of tutors, and a flock of professors couldn't change it, why worry? All I intended to say was that I went through all this twice, leaning heavily on the Unabridged!

From the very start, this book took on a happy life, almost like a song—a rapidly moving cadenza, interspersed with grace notes of divine humor. There was joy in being awakened as fresh as a daisy and feeling the laughter of God searching every part of the temple.

Sometimes I thought well enough of something I had read to copy it for you, and so here is my *2 A.M.* I hope some of the joy I had in writing it permeates your mind and makes the sunrise a little more glamorous.

W.C.L.

Chapter I

Integrity to Instinct

One day I came suddenly and silently from behind a huge evergreen tree and took by surprise a large beige-colored bird.

I stopped, suddenly fascinated by his actions. Instantly he hovered close to the brown earth, near a rock, and tried with all the slender force within him to simulate that thing. It was the only thing he knew how to do. I could see the blessed heart of him fluttering with fear, but he was remaining true to instinct and was doing the only thing he knew how to do at that moment, and that was enough. His fearful eye was watching me, the enemy, but something within him kept saying, "Stay on—it is the only way."

I hastily withdrew to a secluded place where I could watch him. He was not deluded by this decoy but stayed on for five minutes, and then, like a javelin thrown into the air, he rose and flew to freedom.

I was terribly impressed by it all. I remembered many times when I had not been true to my "instinct"—my knowledge, however small, that I was born of God and that I could call upon Him; that I could "having done all, stand" and see and hear and experience the Presence. But the human fear-thing

2 A.M.

was so great that I had often tried to use outside methods to help, and always with small success.

"He shall cover thee with his feathers, and under his wings shalt thou abide"—and a thousand other lovely things—things of "instinct" to adhere to when the sudden thrust of the enemy comes unexpectedly.

Chapter II

A Spinner in the Sun

A large black spider ran swiftly along his elaborate web, suspended in midair between two branches of a swaying willow tree. The early morning sun hit the diadem of dewdrops and made them spurt rainbow lights in a magic circle about his splendid achievement.

He, like some magnificent feudal lord, suddenly let himself glide through space to the far reaches of his domain to reinforce a guy-wire, made a lordly inspection of his estate, and returned as suddenly and as easily as he had descended, to rest in silken dalliance in the center of his universe.

I looked at this masterpiece of engineering. Any master engineer would have been proud to have created a like thing, and yet the spider had drawn it all from within himself. His whole world and way of expression came from within. He unwound his web upon which he was to go, effortlessly traveled blithely over it, and then retrieved it at will.

As I stood there watching the amazing spectacle, the words of Jesus came forcibly to me: "I am the way." The way of *every* man lies within him. Until he discovers that he lays his own way and travels it, he will insist that some outside influence is affecting

2 A.M.

his course in life. This sudden realization that everything has to come from within may jolt the lazy old human thought out of its self-hypnosis; but the sooner it is discovered the sooner will the results take place which he has been seeking for so many years.

How is it that Jesus repeatedly says, "Look within ... ask me ... call upon me ... whatsoever you ask" — and a host of other things — if the resources or the wherewithal from which to produce these things were not there? "Go within ... shut the door," etc. — a thousand and one admonitions are given to find within yourself the thing you are looking for on the outside. Find it first as a reality, as the spider before he plumbs his first line finds the completed web within himself. "I am the way." I AM is the Christ within you, your personal Christ.

Man, having lost his way in the maze of human thought, has failed to hear the words "I am the way" and continues to try to *demonstrate* the way of Life. He is all-unsuspecting that he, too, has within him all that is necessary to "go" anywhere he desires. As with the spider, he has it all within himself, but he keeps trying to get it on the outside.

The moment he discovers this inner resource, he will re-orientate himself and chart his way by the sky map given him by Jesus the Christ.

No man can by thinking do much, but by consciousness and recognition of his divinity, he can find "a way ye know not of"; he can escape the hopeless pattern of human destiny and karmic debt.

He will understand then how it is he must "be still, and know that I am God," and how it also is, "then went he in and shut the door."

Some of the magic of *being* "the way," instead of trying to demonstrate an outside force, is shown in the movements of Jesus, when "instantly he was on the other side of the lake." Can you think that out or make a way by which this would be possible? I believe not—you have to *be* the way. Or can you imagine demonstrating the way through a crowd?

Unless you discover this wonderful capacity, something or somebody is continually blocking your progress; but once you recognize it, then you manifest it. You are the "spinner in the sun." It is wonderful.

"I am the way, the truth, and the light." Your way is within you—chart your own "sky lanes."

Sky Robes

If you are going to descend to the level of criticism and scandal, you must first do as Milton says:

> But first I must put off
> These my sky robes,
> Spun out of Iris' woof,
> And take the weeds
> And likeness of a swain.

You lay aside something beautiful when you criticize and condemn; your heavenly blue and iris robe of Truth must be cast down for the swineherd's rags. Is it worth it? And do you know how long it

2 A.M.

takes to wash your garments clean once you have laid aside your sky robes? Well, try it sometime and see.

There is no jumping back and forth between evil and good. If you believe in evil to the extent that you can make a reality of it in another, you must expect it to gang up on you some day in such force that you will start screaming, "Save me, or I perish." And perhaps someone will hear ... but perhaps not. Watch—be wary about laying off your sky robes. They are very precious.

Chapter III

Flying

Every flyer learns early in his career that his plane must *lift against weight* and *thrust against drift*—lifting against the established laws of the earth plane, in one movement setting aside the old time-honored and unbeatable law of gravity, and then thrusting against the terrible "drift" of the atmosphere, the onslaught of a hundred and one currents, fogs, pockets, and strange, uncharted conditions of the upper sphere.

He lifts because he has a perfectly equipped machine with which to lift, and he thrusts into the unknown and untested atmosphere of a new level by the same power that gave the lift.

There is something remarkably similar between the lifting and thrusting of the plane and the "arising from the pigsty" or the "stretching forth of the hand" or the "opening of the eyes."

There comes a split second after the contact is made when the take-off is necessary—it must be made. The sudden lift is possible because of an even more fast-moving recognition of the possibility of it all taking place. The moment he hesitates and begins examining equipment, he may find it inadequate to

2 A.M.

perform the lift and the thrust, so he either rises or he waits and thinks.

The more a man thinks of the weight of the machine and the law of gravity and the terrible onrush of the vicious and violent currents of air, the more he is convinced that flying is not for him. And so with you—the more you think of your heavy, matter body and mind the more you find it utterly impossible to lift against the old established laws of sin, sickness, and death. When you think of going head-on into the force of human thought with its almost immovable laws, you lose heart and freeze into a mass of human thinking.

There is that instant in prayer—the *click*, the moment when *élan vital* [life force] is struck. In a plane, it is the moment of ignition, when the spark touches the gas and the thing is set in motion. When the Word—quick and instant and "sharper than a two-edged sword" turning in all directions—cuts through the human law of sickness and poverty and sets the marching in motion, it causes it to mount to a new level and make its thrust against all the beliefs of the mortal mind—that wonderful instant when you "hear" and obey, and rise and go.

When Peter asked to come to Jesus, the answer was in the affirmative. Have you noticed that the answers of Jesus were always in the affirmative? He always said, "Yes, whatsoever you will." Having asked for it, you must handle it. So in the case of Peter. He makes his *lift* above established beliefs and is then above the law of gravity, of mortal thinking. He then starts the *thrust* and continues beautifully—until he starts thinking. The moment he starts thinking, the engine is killed, and the machine goes down to the level of what would happen on the thought plane.

Having made your lift and started your thrust, do not look down but keep flying right into the power of God and see the mists of belief disappear, and presently you arrive at the "boat."

You make your lift by the recognition of the Presence and your Divinity within. Once you have made the recognition, something is going to happen; something must happen. Go not back.

"Thrust in the sickle." Do you see the thrust against the human law which says there is no grain to harvest? "Reap where you have not sown." All this wonderful revelation of why the man at the temple gate Beautiful (body) suddenly leaped into the air and praised God and made his thrust into the full activity of the body. You have the equipment within you ready to lift and to thrust and so to fly over human beliefs.

And So He Did

I saw a young boy in the country poking a hornet's nest. I called to him, "Don't do that."

To which he answered, "I want to see what's in it"—and he did!

That curious-looking thing hanging on somebody else's tree had better be let alone unless you want to find out what is in it. Pandora couldn't resist the temptation. Evil has a terrible attraction to the curious.

Subway Talk

Two women were arguing violently in a French Metro station. A third woman approached and entered into the squabble. One of the first women moved away and took her train. Presently another woman came up and joined in. The second of the first group moved away and took her train, leaving the two strange women arguing at blood heat. When last I saw them and the door of the train went closed, they were hard at it, shaking their fists in each other's face. The ones who had started it were far on their way.

"What is that to thee?" is pretty good advice after all! If you are minding your own business, you have plenty to mind—mind you!

Curiosity is the most unspiritual of all the faults of the human mind.

The Plus Value

We have come to a time when we must push up into a degree of consciousness which is *just* beyond that which the average man knows. If we are to "be in this world and not of it," we must know some plus value to life, and this we will know only by appropriation. In writing about this to a friend, I got the following word:

"You spoke of a plus value coming to us, a something just beyond the average understanding of truth. Well, if you push out one leg of the plus sign, you have the cross, and that is probably what Jesus meant when he said, "Take up your cross and follow me."

The cross is just the plus with an elongated leg, and that is why it carries with it such a tremendous power. A *something* beyond the level of the third dimension puts you up into the fourth dimension. The "stretch forth your hand," the "open your eyes," the "look again"—all this is a plus value. Take up your cross and follow Me—the inner Self, the permanent Identity, the Christ.

The Seal of Death
"The seal of death shall be broken, and revelation shall become manifestation."

This is something to contemplate—all the lovely revelation of Jesus Christ shall become literal and actual manifestation. "The kingdom of heaven is at hand" was a revelation. We see it in manifestation from time to time—but imagine it into manifestation for good. All the revelation we have, which sometimes or intermittently comes into manifestation, will be established as a fact.

The blind shall see, the deaf hear, the lame walk, etc.—all of these things and more have we experienced in spots, but *then* it shall be entirely out of the coils of human thought and evil.

2 A.M.

The seal of death will only be broken through the recognition of the Christ within you as Life eternal. "I came that ye might have life, and that ye might have it more abundantly." "I am the truth, the way, and the life." "Come unto me." Blending with this permanent Identity will finally defeat "the last enemy," and then shall we enter into a plane of manifestation and be freed from the coming and going of this lovely truth.

Chapter IV

Painting a Room Green

I decided to paint a room green and decorate it accordingly. The whole action was invisible, inaudible, and unthought of by the world moving around me. The entire transaction had to take place within—the when, the why, the color, and all the rest of it.

The first thing that came up on the outside was something like this: "For the duration," etc., etc., and then followed a string of impossibilities. They were not unlike the impossibilities which confronted Jesus when he had led five thousand into the desert and found they were "murmuring." Can you imagine what the murmurings were like? The same old stuff—"There isn't any bread … why did we come … we are three days away from the city," and so and so and so …

Either you do what Jesus did or your room is not going to be painted green. If you begin to judge from appearances, no matter how time-honored or how well-established, you are not going to "feed the multitude" of human thoughts; so you will have to make your decision and follow the plan of Jesus.

It appears that in spite of all the lack and the impossibility of getting bread and fish, he went within, and whatsoever he performed there was

2 A.M.

"called from the housetops" of manifestation. And so was the room presently painted green.

There is integrity and plenty of mechanics to take place, so "have them sit down in groups of fifty." Why not fifty-one or forty-nine? Well, there is obedience and there is integrity—so make up your mind whether you want to follow what "you" know, see, feel, hear and smell—or what *I* (the Spirit) speaks.

"Stretch forth your hand" and "Look again" is of another dimension than "Well, where are we going to get a painter, paint?" "Bread and fishes?"

"Awake thou that sleepest, and Christ shall give thee light."

Do you want to paint the room green or not?

Chapter V

The Magic Circle

In an old manuscript purporting to come from the Holy of Holies is a description of the magic circle of protection.

The description of it is somewhat after this fashion. When man is called upon to protect himself from seen or unseen forces, he has the power, by *recognizing* his divinity, of casting about himself the magic circle (the description makes one think of a whirling lariat such as Will Rogers made famous), a thing which proceeded out of the temple-body and could be expanded or diminished at will and could be entirely withdrawn. The description says it is a blue-green color, not unlike a neon light, visible to the encroaching evil as well as to the one projecting it.

The projector of this magic circle repeated, as he brought it consciously into being:

"Around myself and mine I throw the ring— 'pass not'—through which naught of evil but only Truth can come to me."

Anything running into this "pass not" circle finds itself devitalized completely and turned back upon itself. All the vicious, evil thoughts and

2 A.M.

attempts of another to injure are turned back upon the sender with accelerated force.

According to the teaching of Jesus, we have many symbols of this same power. We can be surrounded by legions of angels, can entertain the heavenly hosts, find ourselves under the shadow of the Almighty. But this recognition of the magic circle may at times offer an instantaneous means of escape, for it carries with it the suggestion of invisibility. Not that it is going to make you physically nil or invisible, but the force from this Consciousness could make it utterly impossible for the evil thing to find you. "You seek me, but you cannot find me"—yet here am *I* in the midst of you.

Paul speaks about struggling not so much with the flesh as with the powers of darkness, and his protection lay in the recognition of his permanent Identity, "hid with Christ in God."

All of these wonderful ideas are yours for the acceptance of them in *consciousness.* You cannot think your magic circle into existence—it is there the moment you recognize it as true.

Nothing of evil can pass through this magic circle. The moment you *recognize* it, it is into full manifestation. "Stand and see the salvation of the Lord." You are then hid with Christ in God—all of which sounds like so many words until you actually *accept* this new degree of power which has always been yours.

For the sudden thrust of the enemy—"the pestilence that walketh in darkness" or "the destruction that wasteth at noonday"—the only escape is by the recognition of this magic circle of power, which instantly puts to flight the thing called evil.

A Sir Galahad or a Parsifal going forth, shod with the preparation of the gospel—which is a *consciousness of power* and not a religious belief—typifies you when you once come to the place of *belief* in God. Not a profession of the lips and the human thinking mind but a sudden uptilt into Consciousness, into the place of "before ye ask, I will answer." It's yours for the accepting—if you believe in something greater than human thought.

It all sounds like preparation for battle, and yet with this consciousness of the "pass not" you learn to "put up your sword," for "the battle is not yours but God's."

An immeasurable peace comes to you the moment you are conscious of this truth. It will take you through fire and through water and cause you to *come over,* and through hundreds of human complications, in a way you know not of. The old human thought, as undisciplined as a typhoon, finds it cannot go against such a consciousness without committing suicide.

Throughout the literature of the world, inference is made to this magic circle which man possesses and which makes of no account the power of evil.

Milton speaks of it in his poem "Comus." He refers to the power of chastity, that is, singleness of consciousness, recognition of an undefiled state of power.

2 A.M.

> Tis chastity, my brother, chastity:
> She that has that is clad
> in complete steel,
> And, like a quivered nymph,
> with arrows keen,
> May trace huge forests,
> and unharboured heaths ...
>
> What was that snaky-headed
> Gorgon shield
> That wise Minerva wore,
> unconquered virgin,
> Wherewith she freezed
> her foes to congealed stone ...
>
> That when a soul is found
> sincerely so (one-pointed),
> A thousand liveried
> angels lackey her,
> Driving far off each thing
> of sin and guilt.

Virginity—purity of consciousness, recognition of the unsullied mind of God—causes new dimensions to come forth. So we see that pure recognition of your divinity as a reality will apparently destroy the thrusts of the worst combination of human thought. We see the illustration of Minerva's shield, which she gave to Jason; how, when the ugly, snaky-headed monster looked upon its brightness and saw itself for what it was worth, it congealed into stone. Yes, you have power, too, to "pick it up or lay it down," and you have power over all the evil things of the thought world when you but recognize your divinity.

The Magic Circle

Note the line, "A thousand liveried angels lackey her." It is mentioned in the Bible as the heavenly hosts or the twelve legions of angels of which Jesus spoke on the way to the cross.

"Call upon me, and I will answer you" becomes an actual reality when you are established in your own consciousness—"the mind which was also in Christ Jesus."

Arise and awake from the hypnotic thoughts that some force, carnate or discarnate, can touch you. Cast the magic circle of protection about you and see the "pass not" destroy the most terrible human picture ever presented to you. It is wonderful!

In the play "Richelieu" by Bulwer Lytton, we find Richelieu casting this magic circle of protection around his ward, Julie, to save her from the lecherous designs of the dissolute king.

> Then wake the power which in the age of iron,
> Burst forth to curb the great, and raise the low.
> Mark, where she (his word) stands!
> Around her form I draw the awful circle …

The incident proved itself effective since the king was turned back upon himself and departed.

All this dramatic description of the lovely power of the Christ-incident must not cause you to lose sight of the fact that this is a natural, normal capacity of your Christ-Mind—the same Mind which was also in Christ Jesus.

The uses of this revelation are endless, its power so far-reaching. Go within, then, and let it be established in you and understand how it is that "none of these things move me" — nothing can come through. The wonderful circle can only be broken from within, never from without. So take unto yourself the knowledge of this "pass not" circle of protection. It may prove useful many times on the journey.

Wagner has his Brunhilde protected by the magic circle of fire, and while all illustrations are inadequate to give the smallest idea of the revelation, yet they may be enough to cause you to "stand and see the salvation of the Lord."

"The Lord omnipotent reigneth." "Let all the earth be silent before him." Do you begin to *believe* now ... just a little ... perhaps as much as a grain of mustard?

> "Round me and mine I throw the ring 'pass not,' through which naught of evil but only Truth can come to me."

Do you believe? Keep the secret then.

A sheep among wolves passes through unharmed when this secret is understood. You, in the thick of battle, are made invulnerable by the Consciousness.

> Believe in Me, and ye shall be saved.
> Call upon Me, and I *will* answer.

Raising Hell

Aunt Clarissa had a funny way of stating things, which always called to mind that perhaps we do not always *hear* what we hear.

She used to announce, "Well, I'm going to go out and raise hell," when she left for her work in the slums, and in the evening, she always reported that she had raised a good deal of "hell" to heaven that day. There are different ways of raising hell.

Condensation

At the spoken word of Jesus, the invisible became visible—the unseen, unsuspected substance which, like the wind, "bloweth where it listeth," condensed into visible manifestation. The Word is the condenser. When this Word is spoken from the consciousness that I AM THAT I AM, that *particular* I AM— or temple or manifestation—should come into this *particular* situation and disintegrate the congested human thought which has made all sorts of evil pictures.

It is *not* precipitation, which is often referred to as a topflight indication of secret power. It is a natural *releasing* into a plane of physical sight and hearing that which has always been.

You are told to "go thou and do likewise." Does that statement mean anything to you? More study? More seeking? More running to messiahs and leaders, false or true? Or does it carry with it the wonderful realization that when once heard, you can "rise and walk"—and *go* into all the world?"

Does the Word in you mean anything? Are you the Word made flesh, or are you trying to imitate the word of God? Or are you *using* the Word?" Perhaps

2 A.M.

you are still a "reflection" or a "channel" or an "avenue," or some other geographical thing for God to work through.

Or perhaps you have left the Geography Department and gone into the Engineering Division and are now a co-creator with a God, who at the outset said, "It is finished; it is done," and whose greatest purveyor of it all said the same thing. When are you going to *begin*—to commence, to start, to try at least—to *be* the Word in action here and now and shove off from the limited shores of human beliefs? Don't all speak at once.

The Gates of Dawn

"Open! Open, ye gates of dawn—let the Son of man pass through"—the sudden spiritual force which enables you to walk naturally in through the gates and *possess your land*. "They shall go in and come out and find pasture." So it says. What do you say? When will you enter through the gates of dawn into this new dimension of heaven on earth?

All this is done in consciousness, and the moment it is consummated, the outside thing changes. As the gates of a new dawn, or dimension, open to the egg of limited thought, it cracks the shell and finds a new form or level from which to function. Dreaming about the potential things will do no good—there comes a freshness of Life which lifts you out of the morass of human belief and causes you to enter in and be saved.

The gates of dawn are swinging wide open for you. Enter!

Chapter VI

Realm of Manifestation

For some years, the metaphysical world has been gradually stepping out of the field of demonstration into the place of manifestation. To be conscious of a thing is to see it manifest. It is the only level of mind wherein a thing can be "let" through into expression. We are told to get away from the heathenish habit of repeating words, hoping thereby to gain the ear of God. The habit only shows a lack of real faith and posits a belief in mental magic.

When a child becomes conscious of the law of mathematics, he is that law in action, and in order to do "greater things than these," he has to contemplate and magnify the consciousness of mathematics. Then he can with impunity employ this consciousness to disentangle the congestions of human thought called problems.

All problems of whatever nature are made up of thought forms and pictures believed in by man. When a man sets out to write a new arithmetic book, he starts with a full knowledge that the principle of mathematics has no problems. He must therefore invent and superimpose upon his pupils a series of problems made up for the sole reason of proving to the pupil that the answer existed before he made up the problem. The more conscious the pupil becomes of the principle the easier it is to disintegrate the picture problems confronting him. Not by any manner of means would he be taught or think that by repeating a rule—no matter however true—would it work out a problem. He must become conscious of that principle, enter into it, become the law in action, in order to prove his premise that the answer exists before the problem. There is a reason for the faith that is in him, and it is not an emotional, religious, or superstitious sort of thing.

Jesus eternally started with the "it is done" state of mind. From that point, the light of Consciousness penetrated the so-called structure of the problem—whether it was cancer, inharmony, or even death—and as the intensity of this *recognition* continued, the light became so strong that it completely absorbed the darkness of human thought. But this process did not *change* anything. It revealed something that was already done.

"I thank you, Father—I knew this was already done, but I said thank you, for they did not know it was so," or words to that effect. He was working or expressing from the plane of manifestation, or the place of the archetype, the place of the indestructible idea. The archetypal idea of substance (called money on the earth plane) is as unchanging as Life Itself, and to be in that place of manifestation (unmanifest for the moment to the human limited vision and

2 A.M.

understanding) is to cast the reflection or shadow of whatsoever it gazes upon into the realm of matter.

It is both heartening and glorious to start with the premise *it is done,* and especially when you are not trying to *make* that so but are recognizing that it *is* so. At once, the labor or work of prayer is dissipated, and a lovely sense of releasement takes over. "Let the child be born" does away with the labor pains of trying to *make* or create the child.

The affirmation which is true is merely the statement of a fact, unchangeable and eternal. *It is a celestial dimension of mind.* The moment an affirmation is made from that standpoint, a confirmation is on its way to you. How and when it will come depends entirely upon your ability to "believe." Believing is not credulity but your acceptance of the fourth-dimensional consciousness of which Jesus spoke and proved. If you cannot believe—accept and become one with the established facts—you can never see the *eternally existent* answer appear.

So you begin to enter into the realm of manifestation, which you, from a human sense, call the unmanifest but which was created in the beginning and has never changed—and to which nothing can be added and nothing can be taken. In this realm of the finished mystery, you become conscious of the "how much" Jesus showed you in Jerusalem two thousand years ago, and yes, even greater things than these, too, shall you perceive because "there were many things I could not tell you in Jerusalem because of your unbelief."

He did not say he would not tell you when you were ready. For when you are ready, *I* will do the works through you—not maybe or perhaps, but *I will*. It then behooves you to be ready for the works by accepting the beautiful, natural laws of God and getting away from the million and one superstitions hung upon the teaching of the Master as thick as barnacles on a ship a long time from port.

A painter returns often to his model. A copy of a copy of a copy begins to show many divergences from the original, and so we are returning to God and gazing once more on the fair things of creation. Small wonder, then, ye shall "feed among the lilies" and that "ye shall go in and come out and find pasture."

You must, then, enter into the realm of manifestation (unmanifest) and take whatsoever ye will, for it is written, "When ye pray, believe that ye receive (present tense), and it shall be so."

"If ye believe (recognize as finished and done), nothing shall be impossible to you."

"Then went he in and shut the door." Then went he into his own temple, consciousness, and shut the door to opinions and beliefs and prayed the Father—recognized, partook of the bread of heaven. And so I feel it is about time you went in and shut the door and discovered some of the celestial ways and

2 A.M.

means of bringing the manifestation of heaven on earth into view.
    What do you say?

Chapter VII

Light

The closer you follow the inner light of Jesus Christ the more the whole Bible seems to fall apart and reveal its structural form. The superstructure and decorations fastened to the unchanging laws of God are many and often farfetched, but underneath, the *Law* stands. "Underneath are the everlasting arms," the changeless structure of Truth. Jesus always went straight to this. Back of the wretched and decrepit state of man, he found the perfect structure of the created Being which had no capacity to take on any of the evils of the human thinking.

The structure of a skyscraper is straight, uncompromising, unchanging lines of steel. What you put on the outside of this is entirely up to the designer — brick, concrete, stone, and even wood, ornate or plain, enlarged, covered with rococo decorations. And yet the structural thing remains forever the same. Discovering this, one has a basis to work from instead of the outside appearance. And so with man; when he discovers this permanent Identity, he experiences a thrill of delight that his feet are at last planted on an unchanging thing.

Hidden under all the parables and stories of the Bible are these unchanging laws of Spirit. Presently,

2 A.M.

as you begin to dig away the story with its padding, you discover the reality back of it. Hence, the command "Go into a city and there meet a man ... and he will lead you to an upper chamber where the banquet is prepared" reveals its secret doctrine, its unchanging law. A city is a state of consciousness, and since it is a strange city (one you have not yet entered), it is new and clean and fresh. Entering into this new state of consciousness, into this place of virgin consciousness, you can superimpose upon it the desires of your heart.

Presently, when this has been done, when you have "taken" your good—when you have prayed in accordance with the Law—the man is met. Just what this man is going to be, no one knows, nor *how*, *when*, or *where* you are suddenly going to be let into the complete fulfillment of your desire, which you have superimposed (accepted) on the virginal consciousness of pure acceptance. But "meet a man" you surely will. An idea, an urge, a something will come along and start the assembling of the body of the new consciousness.

At the moment of conception, or recognition, it begins to take place. It has sent forth its invisible power to draw that which is necessary to bring out the body with which to clothe itself. Otherwise it remains an unborn thing—a thing without a body, a symbolical manifestation, worthless and of no import.

Once you have actually accepted your desire as a present reality, something begins to happen. Ways

Light

and means that ye know nothing of begin to come to your aid. Unexpected, unheard, and undreamed of things begin to give you a sign. You meet the man, and he will lead you to the upper room of fulfillment where the banquet is prepared for you, or the manifestation has taken place.

Remember that it is the "impossible" you are seeking, for you have already brought out all that is "possible" at this stage of evolution. If it were possible, you would do it; but what you seek is apparently impossible; and there is only one way this can take place, and that is by the power of Almighty God, stepped down through your Divinity—Christ (permanent Identity or Father within)—and finally congealed or condensed into a visible form through your temple-body. Even as invisible vapors can be put through the machinery of a distilling and freezing plant and handled with your hands, so can it also be sent back into the invisible. So can you disintegrate anything and cause it to go back to its native elements.

When you arrive at last at the banquet room, you there "eat my body (substance) and drink my blood (inspiration)" and throw the skeleton away. In other words, you enter into your new manifestation; you use it, enjoy it. It is wonderful!

On entering into the city (new state of consciousness) whereupon you are superimposing your desire, you are cloaked with silence and secrecy. No one must know the moment of conception. Thou fool, do you not know that "a seed must first fall in the ground and rot before it shall be made alive." Trying to superimpose your new desire upon the mind that is filled with disbelief and wonder brings nothing but a blurred, confused manifestation at best. It must be a clean and new state of consciousness—a new sheet of paper, a new level into which you enter. It is wonderful!

Off With Her Head

The Queen of Hearts said, "Off with her head," and Alice was about to succumb to a fit of terror, when all of a sudden she discovered something. "Why," she said, "you're nothing but a pack of cards," and with that, they all flew away.

Sometimes in your ongoing, you come to just such an impasse, where faith seems to be nothing but a sort of snow blindness without rhyme or reason, and the whole pack of human thoughts array themselves against you; and then, all of a sudden, the vision gets its extension, and you see through. And so, "look again" and see the time-space thing telescoped into the *now*.

Man Has Worked Out Many Inventions

But he has created nothing. For instance, what bread machine or high-powered bakery could turn out five thousand loaves in five minutes, to say nothing of the fleet of fishing boats needed to accompany this output with freshly roasted fish? What high-powered machine of any description can take you

Light

"instantly on the other side of the lake"? What manner of thought transference of invention can heal the servant "in the selfsame hour"?

So think on these things and push out the borders of your tent a little. The *created* man is beginning to appear in you, and he knows all these things as natural and easy. The man born of woman is of few days and full of trouble—is that enough?

Yes, man has worked out many "inventions" and can kill himself with most of them, no matter how wonderful they are.

Be Sure You Hear What You Hear

Our wonderful Amelia Earhart said, when she met the ex-Prince of Wales and was asked what she thought of him, "He is exactly as I thought he would be," which amounts to saying exactly nothing as far as the listener is concerned. But two or three writers reported this statement as if Miss Earhart had said, "He was wonderful." Maybe she did mean that—but *listen* and see what you hear when one speaks.

So Much Fortune-telling

So many people who are supposed to be prophets are merely advising their clients, "What you should do is this," but the client again hears, "You are going to do so and so." Stop, look, and listen. I said, "Stretch forth your hand." Can you hear that? Or, "Rise and walk" or, "Open your eyes." I am not

2 A.M.

advising; I am giving you the power to do it—if you can take it.

The Greeks Had a Word for It

The ancient Hebrews had seventy-two names for God and used them definitely in their prayers, in connection many times with the Psalms. There is something mystic in the command *"in my name,"* and when you begin to examine into this multi-named Deity, it is not so remote as it may seem. We find ourselves praying to a God of love, a God of strength, a God of substance, decision, faith, etc. There is something powerful about concentrating the entire attention on a single, given phase of God.

The Greeks divided this universal Power into twelve main branches and called upon the god representing the particular quality they desired to see into manifestation. They prayed to Aphrodite as definitely as you pray to God as Love, and at this time, if we had been under the order of ancient Greece, no doubt during this war we would pray to Mars, just as we pray to the All-powerful Deity for victory.

It is interesting, therefore, to give some attention to this angle of prayer and examine a little into the nature of the name you are calling upon. There is something direct, clean-cut in decision; it is a force that cuts off all extraneous ideas and thoughts; just as there is a relaxing consciousness which goes with agreement and a warmth of feeling that comes from praying to God as Love.

There may be as many names as seventy-two, if we were to count them, but the single-track purpose of reaching that quality of God necessary to see manifested at the moment I believe is somewhat aided and abetted by singling out the particular name of God and aligning ourselves with God as that.

God as the universal, everywhere-present substance is somewhat nebulous—like the wind that "bloweth where it listeth ... and no man knoweth whither it cometh and whither it goeth." It is, therefore, possible for you to deify Him in one of his attributes, and when you go within your closet and pray for love, the ensuing manifestation must and will be in the nature of Love.

The multiplicity of ideas that always follows will likewise be in the nature of the "name."

Prayer is the capacity to recognize God—the power to align yourself with the Presence and the Power, which results in manifestation. "When ye pray, believe that ye shall receive, and it shall be so." When you pray for success by recognizing God as success, then it is success that will come to you. The quality of the name-nature will take on a body and form.

The Reason

Did you ever question how it was that the servant of the centurion was healed? Was it just a happenstance?

2 A.M.

Do you know of any general who would go across a continent to ask for help for his servant?

Servants and slaves were cheap in those days. One more or less wouldn't have done much to the family budget; and yet we find this centurion, gorgeous in his scarlet and gold, a man who had proved his worth by actual combat, coming miles (and miles were longer in those days of no airplanes) to ask for help for a servant.

Ever imagine that it was the love of this centurion for his servant that might have opened the way for instantaneous relief? There was not only authority in both of these men (Jesus and the centurion) who met, but there was love, and since "perfect love casteth out fear," so does it cast out the results of fear—disease.

Ouch, Sir

"Ouch, Sir" said the young sergeant who was being decorated by the colonel before his regiment. The colonel evidently didn't know how thin the jacket of the sergeant was, and the sergeant had to be polite—what a terrible situation. Just like the metaphysician who is always *holding a thought*. The longer you hold it the worse the situation gets. If you want it to work, let it go. If you want a seed to grow, throw it away. Your seed must change shape, and it can never accomplish this as long as you hold it. Neither can a thought get into manifestation as long as you "hold" it.

"Ouch, Sir,"

I'm so sorry if it upsets your applecart of antiquated metaphysics—hope there weren't many apples in it.

A Discovery

A noted psychiatrist recently said people who are interested in the sex lives of other persons are motivated by one of three reasons—they are either repressed, suppressed, or repulsed.

He also said when they speak of having a "friend" who is doing this, that, or the other thing, it is more than likely they are speaking about themselves.

When they ask a question, it is generally because they know the answer and want to while away a little time in a useless fashion.

When they ask advice, it will not be taken.

So let your conversation be, "Yea, yea" and "Nay, nay." When they see the light and call, you will hear and answer, and *that* will be *that*. "My sheep hear my voice"—others do not matter, so follow Me.

Confirmation

The moment an *affirmation* is made, it travels directly to its *confirmation*. The reason one makes an affirmation is that the confirmation is already established. The reason you pray or affirm a truth is because that which you are praying for is pressing towards you for expression, and that is why you make the affirmation. It is a statement of a fact—

already established in God, awaiting your willingness to *let* it be confirmed into manifestation.

Having been warned about repetition of words, you will see the difference in saying over and over pretty statements of truth and in *stating a fact*. "Before you ask ..."—prayer from this standpoint is an established fact.

I feel almost certain that the affirmation-confirmation of Life eternal was tried out in the case of Lazarus. Being the closest associate of the Master, it is reasonable to believe that he knew many things regarding the Power which escaped others. It would have only been in line, then, for Lazarus to offer himself as a sort of human guinea pig, a chance to see whether he could self-resurrect since they both knew that Jesus was going to undergo this same test.

Jesus was to be absent from Lazarus when he died, and in the event he could not *self-resurrect*, or find his own confirmation of Life eternal, then Jesus would come and speak the Word into being.

I was pleased, therefore, when I ran upon mystic Homer Cook believing in the same idea.

The affirmation has its confirmation, and if it cannot come through the opacity of your own mind, then another will bring it to you; so watch. *To every affirmation there is a confirmation.*

"What Went Ye Out for to See?"

Few there be who can accept the inspiration without taking the superstitions and limitations of

Light

the teacher. The purple and fine linen are so obvious by their presence or by their lack.

"Blessed art thou when men shall curse you and revile you."

Do you believe that? Then what are you making such a fuss about all the evil stories and things said about you? If it is an indication of a *blessing,* then you should *rejoice.* And that is the trick that suddenly bursts the shell of the cursing and releases the beautiful full-feathered bird of paradise.

More Blessings
"The wrath of man shall (not maybe or perhaps) bless you." Well, what's the matter? Why don't you demand it, if that is a law? Rejoice and be glad, for your redeemer draweth nigh.

"No (not any) weapon that is formed against thee shall prosper." Pretty hard on the poison pens of anonymous letters and the violent wagging tongues. Wait and see. If you know this, you will see. So rejoice.

Because he has placed his trust in Me (isn't it wonderful when you ponder it all? Can you do it?), "the gates of hell shall not prevail" against you—and so *because* …

"I bring not peace, but a sword" to all this evil thing which tries so unceasingly to destroy you. And so …

I am the avenging angel, and vengeance is mine. Well, forget the hurt. All the accounting is done on

2 A.M.

the other side—and statements are sure to be sent out on the first of the month.

Chapter VIII

The God within You

The involuntary action in your body is God within you in action. The voluntary action is largely engendered by thought.

As long as the body is controlled by involuntary action, it is harmonious and largely out of mind. The moment the voluntary action of thought takes over, evil begins to appear.

If, for instance, the thought imagines it sees a snake and takes over, the entire organism is affected. If the fear is great enough, it will kill the body through fear thus engendered.

Human thought, or voluntary action, could not have brought forth an Immaculate Conception. The moment the idea which is of God is touched by thought, it disappears.

Since My (God's) ways "are past finding out," the less thought that is given to the involuntary functioning of this power the better. "To be absent from the body and present with the Lord" is suggested as the formula for perfect health.

The blending, then, with the Lord within—the magnifying of this in consciousness, free from thought, the "feeling" after Me instead of "thinking" after Me—is the key to all healing. The moment you

2 A.M.

become one with this automatic, involuntary Power within a patient, the thought (voluntary) pictures begin to disintegrate, no matter what their origin or intensity.

Nothing can stand in the way of this recognized God within, for that is the Life force, the point where It is actually in manifestation. To recognize this as an already established thing will cause it to "enlarge the borders of its tent" to a degree which will absorb the supposed action of thought. Healing is only a matter of recognizing Christ as actually within. Nothing can defeat this Power once recognized; even death can be made to disappear.

There is no way of transforming yourself, which you are told to do, by the conscious thought. A slight betterment may take place, but it is negligible. But "by the renewing of your mind" (consciousness of the Christ within) one begins to see Light.

The Christ within, then, is the actual Life of man, the literal existence of him, and It is already in manifestation, even though It appears to be functioning in a definite evil way. It is the eternal identity of man and cannot be destroyed. That is why you are told to "raise the dead." You are only raising a dead thought.

Suffering from maladjustments and internal bodily trouble, the path of freedom lies within the recognition of this automatic, involuntary Power already there. The dropping of everything from thought and the entering into this *recognition* will right the condition with the speed commensurate to your recognition, and, rising from a sick bed, you will be able to say with authority, "I am well" and mean it.

This automatic Power within you knows everything and can do everything, but the moment the voluntary thought gets hold of you, it claps you into a prison house of limitation. Even in the "thought" praying, it finally becomes exhausted and cannot give the perpetual adoration—the "pray without ceasing" it is commanded to do—but falls of sheer exhaustion. But when you enter into the Life within, you automatically pray without ceasing, for it is a constant flood of praise and recognition of the Presence.

You begin to see, then, that man has no "health" of itself; he has a consciousness of Life which manifests in a degree of health necessary to carry out the instructions of this involuntary Power within. This Power within, this Christ, is the point of contact with the unseen, the place where the invisible is *stepped down* to manifestation. "The kingdom of heaven has come nigh unto you," and the keys of healing have been actually placed in your hands. It is well!

Chapter IX

Increase

"And Satan stood up against Israel, and provoked David to number Israel," notwithstanding the fact that Joab said to him, "The Lord maketh a hundred times so many more as they be."

But David insisted. He had to know to the last man and to the last bit of material just what he had to count on, disregarding the invisible increase which can and does "maketh a hundred times so many more than they be."

The whole revelation of Jesus Christ is based on the increase, sometimes ten and sometimes a hundred and sometimes a thousandfold—that is, when the measure has not been stepped down to a certain quantity. If you only have a pint measure and you know it, what good to have a hundred times more liquid than will fill it? And so when you step your universe down to that which you can count and handle with your hands and circumscribe with the human knowledge—what good to pray for increase?

"Open, ye gates of dawn, and let the Lord pass through," the inward flow of the invisible substance which maketh it a hundred or thousand times more than is evident on the surface. If you count your soldiers and find them to be materially less than those of your enemy, what is the natural conclusion? Defeat of course. And so with everything else in life. Trying to demonstrate wealth while you know positively that all you have is a certain limitation is one of the quickest ways to frustration and will result in the old cliché, "Well, I never did think this thing worked."

The wrath of God on David for his failure to accept the "twelve legions of angels" or the increase ("look again, the fields are white") is only the light of God disintegrating the false law of Satan (human thought).

"What have ye in your house?"

"Three drops of oil, a handful of meal."

"Well, disregard it at once and start pouring, and borrow measures not a few."

"What? With only three drops of oil?"

No—that question brings the wrath of God down upon your head, which is merely the forsaking of you to your own devices.

With your mental eyes glued upon the manifest realm, how are you to experience the increase? Where is it coming from, and where are you going to put it if you only have a pint cup—which you positively know is all that you have?

"You (still?) say it is four months to the harvest." Is that what you say? Still professing to be a Truth student? Your human eyes will never see it, and you will never experience it, until you have come fully to the acceptance of the Presence here, there, and everywhere—*awaiting recognition*. Then when you

2 A.M.

go forth, no matter if your enemy has a thousand and more soldiers than you, the invisible Presence will take care of all that, in "a way you know not of." Do not try to find out—only *believe*. Take your attention away from the manifestation. "Be absent from the body and present with the Lord."

"Faith is the substance of things hoped for, the evidence of things not seen." Recognition of the Presence puts you in a "sense-feel" state of consciousness which can and does release the "twice as much as he had before" and will fill everything that is empty in your life—unless you insist that you only have a pint measure. Then, of course, if the whole Niagara Falls passed over the cup, you would only have a pint.

The moment you step yourself down to appearances, you come under the law of judging from appearances, which at best is a great limitation and which proves without a shred of doubt that you never did believe in God—that is, the God of Jesus —but rather in a limitation of human thinking, a man-god, with all his foibles and limitations.

Recalling again the "Satan stood up against Israel and provoked David to number Israel"—the next time you have a desire to count your limitations before entering into prayer, cast this idea from you with the blessed recognition that "the Lord maketh his people a hundred times more as they be." Note the present tense of the verb—the Lord, the recognition of the Presence, *makes* it take place in the *present* tense.

Stop Counting Your Soldiers

Stop numbering Israel and start counting your blessings—starting, of course, with the three drops—and they will be as the sands of the sea. When the dam or obstruction of looking to appearances is once broken, the River of Life will flood the desert of your life, and it will blossom as a rose. "The Lord maketh (not maybe or perhaps) his people a hundred times more as they be." Is that enough? Do you believe? Well, why don't you answer me?

But—If

"But if I could only see an immortal, I would believe in immortality."

"Well, I'm sorry. You're never going to see an immortal until you arrive at immortality yourself. Until you *believe* and become conscious of immortality, you will never experience it, for it would be impossible for you to see immortality with a mortal conscience.

"What thou beest, that thou seest." This old adage holds true today as of yore. Whatever you are in consciousness, you see manifested automatically all about you. When you become conscious of immortality, you will see plenty of immortals all about you; and inversely, when you are sick, you eventually enter into a place where you see sickness all over the place.

2 A.M.

"Come out from among them (the human thoughts) and be free." It is no good tying to "work" some system of truth to bring about immortality. You will suddenly discover it when you believe and do not *try* to believe. There will be oceans of manifestations of any state of consciousness into which you enter. Remembering, then, that "in my Father's house are many mansions (many degrees of on-going), you will begin to push forward—you will begin to "launch out into deeper waters." You will begin to try your wings for a skyward flight. You will put on the garments of Light—your sky robes. You will mount up with eagle wings.

Knowing, then, that you are not going to be given a sign, it behooves you to enter in and shut the door and find out some of the realities of Life, which will cause you to shed the rags of impoverished human thinking.

"Prove me, and see if I will not open windows in heaven (your consciousness) and pour out a blessing you cannot receive." Why cannot you receive it? Because it is so much greater than your human mind has ever dreamed of. It says "prove me"—but don't you dare *try* to prove Me to see whether it will work or not, for it will not work. You prove a thing from a recognized state of consciousness.

So maybe sometime you will see immortals all over the place; that will be heaven, which Jesus said is within you—and here and *now*. Can you take it?

Chapter X

In a Dream—In a Vision

"Your young men shall dream dreams, and your old men shall have visions."

I have had many dreams and visions which were subsequently fulfilled. The only danger in speaking of the subject is the mistaken understanding in the meaning of the words. To think for a moment that every jumbled or passing dream has meaning is to also believe that every passing thought is an inspiration from God.

One can become so caught in the mystery of interpreting dreams as to become entirely bemused when a real, meaningful dream or vision comes. The interpretation of a dream generally comes *with* the dream or soon after, so that the searching for "dream book" meanings to the symbols given is ridiculous. When the meaning is not forthcoming, one has only to ask, *believing*, and the interpretation will come to light.

Of the hundreds of dreams and visions which carried through to manifestation, none were more interesting or more satisfying than the two following:

One night I dreamed the word *trilogy*. It was so clear and spoken with such force that I awakened and jotted it down on a pad and went back to sleep.

2 A.M.

The next night, the word came again, and this time with a quotation from the Bible, which was spaced so that it would make the titles of three books. "I Came ... That Ye Might Have ... Life More Abundant" — then sleep again. The third night, I awakened again, with the urge or command to write three books. At the time, I was lecturing ten times a week, but when the Power, or revelation, started on its way to manifestation, nothing could stop it—and so in the five short weeks allotted me, I found the three books completed. The dream, or revelation, had become manifestation.

Another night, I dreamed the name *Mythra*. I looked it up and found it to be the name of the Assyrian sun goddess. The following night, the image of a smoke-gray Persian cat with a dark face came with the name. Six weeks later, in going through the pound with a friend, I paused in front of one of the cages—and looking at me was the cat seen in the dream.

I took her out of her box. She put her arms around my neck and fastened her claws into my coat collar. Neither the attendant nor I could get them loose, and so she came home with me to live with tawny K. O. and Black Lilac (two cats) and jade-green Gurli, the South American parrot. They made a beautiful splash of color and animation when together.

It wasn't long before we found Mythra to be a very unusual cat. She seemed to want to get under any cloth lying about, and so Rose made her a little blanket which she accepted with glee, purring and looking up with her large emerald eyes. This led to other clothes and hats, until she was as beautifully furbished as a fashionable night club singer. This little bundle of Love brought hours of joy and entertainment into the home. Li'l old Mythra, a dream come true.

Chapter XI

It Is Consummated

One night about 2 A. M., I was awakened from a profound sleep. It was almost as if I had not been to bed at all, so complete was the awakening.

I got up, went into the bathroom and took a shower, and went out into the garage, where I had a box of soft clay.

I had been working for some weeks on the idea of *embodiment*—that is, personifying the thing you are doing—and as a result of this had brought home a box of clay, attempting after a fashion to *let* something take place through me, something which was entirely outside my ordinary capacities. My success had been more or less mediocre—not exactly disappointing but not too flattering.

I took a handful of clay and found myself modeling a sort of crude cross, at the top of which I sketchily put in INRI, the jest which the clowning human mind had placed on the original cross— "Jesus, the King of the Jews."

Then the thought came to me to make a crucifix, but immediately I was startled by the idea of anything so terrific as molding a likeness of our Lord. I felt unworthy to attempt such a job and sat holding the clay. Almost as if by magic, I looked down and

It Is Consummated

found my hands sort of closing in on a slender body; my fingers seemed to be modeling the clay almost unconsciously. A surprisingly beautiful body lay there. I looked at it with such tender affection that tears came to my eyes, and I realized that I had to lay it on the cross. Some way or other, for a moment, I sensed the fact that everybody had to crucify Jesus, the wonderful symbol of materialized Spirit.

I fastened his hands to the arms of the cross and put my hand under his precious head—when suddenly the whole figure crumpled up and fell half away from the cross. In doing so, the weight was almost entirely suspended by the left arm; and clay seemed more like rubber than anything else, and the muscles of the back and chest came into being. It seemed as if the left arm would be torn from its socket—the head dropped on the breast, and I knew "it was consummated."

For a while, I stared down at the thing that had happened, and then I started to reach for some tools to work out more of the details on the unfinished hands and feet—but something restrained me, and so I left it unfinished as it was.

The next morning when I saw it again, I was glad I had not gone further but had left it as it had come through. God has wondrous ways which are past finding out—and past trying out. The restraining influence of the power flowing through a musician playing so much faster than his human mind can work, through all the intricacies, indicates what

2 A.M.

must and will take place in us when we will "let that mind be in us which was also in Christ Jesus."

"It is consummated." The eventual giving up of all struggle and the entering into the heritage which awaits you will release many wonderful things through you.

A few days after the crucifix had been cast and some copies made of it, a friend found these lovely lines coming through about it:

> The man of sorrow walked his lonely path;
> And then, his listening heart
> Thrilled to, "My Son;"
> No cruel deed, nor vicious wrath,
> Can harm *the One*.
>
> —Andrea Higgin

Profanity

"Thou shalt not take the name of the Lord thy God in vain, for the Lord thy God will not hold him guiltless who taketh his name in vain."

Every negative and evil thing that you attach to your I AM is taking the name in vain. When you say "I am sick," you have taken the Name/Nature in vain, for the I AM cannot experience the illusion of human thought called sickness. Illusion? Yes, witness Moses putting his hand into his bosom and taking it out white with leprosy—and again putting it in his bosom and taking it out clean.

It Is Consummated

You are not going to argue, are you? Well, not unless you are still thinking that the human intellect has something to do with God.

It is so, or it is not so.

Jesus is a truthsayer or a liar.

"Choose ye this day whom you will serve."

The terrible railing against what the world calls profanity, while in the same breath the Name/Nature of God is taken in vain, is childish and accomplishes nothing.

"Thou shalt have no other gods before me." There is only *one* God in consciousness—*millions* in thought.

"Etoile Filante Qu'il Faut Saisir au Vol"

"Shooting star which one must grasp in flight." So it is with the lovely inspiration which, like the wind, "bloweth where it listeth." The sudden inrush of Spirit that comes at certain times—the flash, the quick spurt of light in the midnight of human thinking—that is the shooting star which one must trap in its flight.

A Fig for You

A fig tree is supposed to bear figs. And if it doesn't ... well? But you say it is not the season. The fig tree is supposed to bear figs. There is no season in God; it is always the fullness of the Presence—that is, if you can see it. It does not look to the botanist to find out when a flower will bloom. "Ye shall find the plant before the seed," and so ... can

2 A.M.

you step it up a little and *see*? "There was no rain or man to till the soil," and yet ...

And Again:
Prayer is conception—the masculine knowing touches the feminine feeling, and the new idea starts immediately to take unto itself a body and form.

The heat of an incubator must be kept steady and unvarying, and so must your contemplation of the "it is done" state of things which is to bring it out.

"I have never (and that is a long time) seen the righteous begging bread." No use arguing—you know the answer.

Meditation:

> A citadel of calm ... divine tranquility ... a fathomless sea; voices ... color, cadences ... perfume of words ... dramatic pauses.

The swine of human thinking go over the cliff of oblivion. You go over the abyss of eternity—to find your wings.

The highest reaches of Truth are the simplest recognition of the Presence.

That you exist is enough to make you know you are eternal.

Righteous Indignation
And then there comes a time when the righteous indignation rises within you, and you *rise* and smite the rock and make it give forth the waters of Life.

Ever watch a dog come out of the water? The first thing he does is give himself a good, vigorous shake.

Why not try it? Give yourself a good, vigorous mental and physical shake and rid yourself of a lot of barnacles that have slowed you down.

Chapter XII

Let God Let

The magic came to me at last—I discovered I was to "let God let."

Somewhere hidden away in this line came the remembrance of *letting*—the "God spake" thing, "Let there be light, and there was light," and when the whole manifest creation proceeded in orderly fashion, all of it appearing by the magic of the word *let*—and this further alignment of *letting* yourself *let* God takes on a new and interesting meaning.

You cannot *make* God do anything. In some places, Jesus did not many mighty works—not because the Power was absent but because the people could not "let" it take place. In other words, they could not let themselves go to the point of *letting* God manifest through the human belief.

"Let there be light"—and there was light. There was neither sun, moon, nor stars (all symbols of the Light) created as yet. And then, too, there were the plants in the field and no rain yet and no one to till the soil. When we are speaking of this God-power, it is not something measured by human thought. It reverses all science regardless, for it is above the laws of cohesion, adhesion, gravity, and limitation. Read for yourself and see.

Let God Let

The moment an invisible thing is slowed down to a point of visibility, which we call matter, it begins to disappear. The moment you drive a car from the dealer's half a block, it is a used car; disintegration sets in immediately, and the manifestation is only held in place by your consciousness of it. The moment you drop it from consciousness, it begins to fall apart or disappear. That is why the command "loose him and let him go" is so important to you. What you hold in consciousness stays put until you loose it and let it go, and then it *has* to go.

When you withdraw consciousness from anything, the process of disintegration is very rapid. A house which is closed up, though protected by every possible device, starts to fall to pieces. The furniture will go down in tone. Why? Because there is no *conscious life* there. You see how your world of manifestation depends upon your consciousness. No wonder, then, Jesus counseled, "Be still, and know that I am God."

This all brings you to the place of "releasement." You begin to *release* your good instead of trying to make it appear. What a heavenly word to return to Jehovah. Since "heaven and earth are full of thee" (the substance), there is plenty to release.

Release the love of God through your temple-being and see it flood the world of yours with Light.

For forty years, their garments and shoes "waxed not old." Shows what consciousness does compared to the human law of life. "Come then—let us reason together."

2 A.M.

Assumption

The word *assumption* is better understood through the feeling than by the hearing. It is a gradual merging of one substance into another, a sort of osmosis, just as alcohol absorbs, and is absorbed by, the oil of a flower and produces a third substance, perfume. It is nothing that can be forced; when the point of saturation is reached, it is complete. The assumption of your God-given heritage, which became almost completely separated from you, is not by sudden flight but by a gradual infiltration of the consciousness you are recognizing as immortal.

Jesus invited this assumption and said, "The works I do, ye shall do also, and even greater." As you begin to see this recognition, which eventually results in assumption of that virginal mind, you will also begin to recognize that in a more or less degree this assumption has been going on for some time.

If you assume a thing as true, such as perfect health or wealth or what you will, you do not try by hook or crook to make a demonstration, but begin such a "letting" process into manifestation that before you know it, you detect, as in the analysis of perfume, the aroma of the flower rising in clouds from the mixture of oil and alcohol. So is matter merging with Spirit into that third substance, *flesh*— "yet in my flesh shall I see God"—and you begin to prepare to *see* God in a thousand and one ways and

Let God Let

degrees that never could have happened before. You begin to see God in the flesh—in the new assumed state of consciousness. It is wonderful!

At that point, you assume the various phases of God. You heal not because you try to heal but because you cannot do anything else. The moment another person *sees* this Light and calls upon you, the Light lengthens and intensifies Its power to a degree that is above the degree of the human congested thought which is producing the difficulty in the other. It is nothing you do; once you have made this assumption, it is something you cannot help doing. "Who touched me, for I perceive that virtue (healing) has gone out of me." And so it goes.

The *assumption* of your Christ-power—the mind which was also in Christ Jesus—does not bring importance, self-aggrandizement, etc. It brings a sense of integrity of purpose but withal a *standing* or a resting in the consciousness, leaving the results entirely to the osmosis or the permeation of the Light.

"Come to me" requires not only a decision but a complete assumption above human thinking and laws before a heavier-than-water body can venture out onto its surface.

The assumption of Light dissipates the density of matter laws and beliefs. The assumption of the virgin—the pure, unadulterated acceptance of your Christ-Consciousness—will bring much into manifestation which has been hidden, lo these many years.

2 A.M.

Genius

Genius is your capacity to know God. In God, man finds the sum total of all talent, waiting to be expressed. If he can fix his recognition on this, he will sidestep the limitations of human thinking.

We see the so-called child prodigy solving problems with ease which stump a great mathematician. Why? Does he think? Apparently not. In a flash, he has the answer—because the answer already exists. "Before you ask, I will answer." The key word is "Do you *believe*?" Not, "Do you try or want or wish to believe?" Do you *believe* in God?

The more you *stay* your power on the principle of Life the greater the interest accruing. Looking straight into the face of God causes you to die to some of the limitations of human thought. Hence, we see a child of three playing a difficult concerto. His physical equipment is many times inadequate to the Power he has released through his temple. "Come and let us reason together."

Ye men of Athens, "know ye not that ye are gods?" Know ye not that the very attributes and powers you are embodying in a marble statue are actually in you—awaiting recognition, awaiting the purity of consciousness which can "believe." Mary magnified the Power within her, and the child was set on earth. You contemplate the law of mathematics or music and you increase perceptibly in the expression, and the more you contemplate it the more the expression comes forth—the more natural it becomes.

There are ten talents, if you can take them.

Chapter XIII

They Say

From the quiver of human mind, the most poisonous dart of all is labeled, "They say."

One day, after a very illuminating lecture on God-Love, a woman came to me and asked for a few moments. Not being in the habit of giving interviews, I told her so, but she persisted and clung to me and finally forced her attentions on me by walking with me to the car. What she had to say ran something like this:

"Of course, Mr. Lanyon, far be it from me to speak anything evil about another, but I feel it is my duty to warn you that the lady I saw you with yesterday after the lecture—well, "they say" she has broken every one of the ten commandments but one."

I looked at her. Her otherwise rather nice-looking features were drawn down into the mask of a sensuous monster—her eyes slimmed, her lips tightened. She was the embodiment of the murderess, yet she would protest that she could not kill a chicken for dinner.

All I said to her, which incensed greatly, was "Well, Madam, you are trying to break that *one*—why don't you use a knife?"

They Say

What did all the stupid, repressed, and suppressed ladies do with the "bad order" they had on their hands after Jesus had asked them, "He that is without sin, cast the first stone"? I wonder. Do you? Well, some of them had a lifetime job trying to get rid of that which Mary Magdalene dropped off like a soiled garment. Unconsciously, they had cast lots for her robe—and got it. But what to do with it? Rather a difficult situation, especially to a respectable man or woman.

Remember that *everything*—a lovely fourth-dimensional word—everything goes into the kingdom of heaven before the scandalmonger. Are you going to get in?

The other morning on the way to the lecture, a man waiting at a bus stop asked if he might ride. He did. Hardly had he gotten in the car before he started a filthy story about a prominent Hollywood star who was making the headlines in a rather unsavory light. He spewed his venom all over the place. When he finally came to a period in his talk, I asked him if he knew the person he was talking about. "Well, no, not exactly, but my wife has a cousin who works in the cutting department of the studio, and a girl told her!" I watched the expression on his face in the mirror. Gradually his upper lip extended; his teeth seemed to distend like fangs. The rattle of his filthy mind made the picture perfect—coiled, ready to strike.

Weeks after, the person was exonerated, and I wondered of that one, what he has done with the

2 A.M.

"bad order" he set out into the world as a reality—for it was a positive reality to him, and he would have to handle it from that standpoint.

"They say." I have often asked the holier-than-thou one who was carrying the precious news who "they" were. Ah, that is where the great Christ-Love comes to the front. "I wouldn't think of betraying a confidence—I couldn't tell who said it."

No, neither could the friends of Judas betray his confidence—and so the beautiful manifestation of God-Love went on her way, to see if she could "demonstrate" a healing of a cancer or leprosy or some other little trifle that might feed upon just that sort of thing.

It is wonderful how the Power takes care of these scandalmongers, and now that the new descent of Light is here, the reaction will be more direct and effective—praise God for that—for they must learn not to "despise the chastening of the Lord."

It is wonderful!

Wind

As the wind ripples, rustles, thrills, and sometimes shrieks through the trees, it becomes a symphony played by nature in one of her happy, carefree moods.

"The wind bloweth where it listeth," and no man knoweth, yet man can experience it. So it is with the Spirit of God.

When Consciousness is recognized, old words are changed and have new meanings. Traveling under the lash of *delusion,* of a life where everything worked in reverse—"when I would do good, evil I do," etc.—suddenly, through recognition, *delusion* became *illusion*. The sting and curse had been removed, and once having seen this transformation, the *illusion*, or veil itself, is ready to be rent.

Note the strange alliteration in words of a common meaning—home, heaven, health, happiness, halcyon on the positive side, and hate, hell, harm, heinous, etc. Give this a little time and see what magic there is in words.

"Take words ... and return to Jehovah." Try a letter—peace, plenty, power, and poverty; pain, perplexity, etc." Yes, take words and return to Jehovah and set them on fire and find out what is inside of them.

The End of an Illusion

> Death is nothing but the end of an illusion.
> —Talbot Mundy

Paul said, "I die daily," and it is wonderful to understand that this daily dying is only the end of another illusion, and finally the last enemy shall be completely overcome and the illusion of death in the body-temple will be swallowed up—will be found to be merely just the end of an illusion.

Now

"Now is the accepted time; now is the day of salvation." It is always *now*, and it is *now* or never. That which was, now is, and none can change it. That which was not, is not; none can bring it into being. That which shall be, *now* is, or it could never be.

"Where there is no vision, the people perish." Where there is no vision of the complete, finished mystery, the "before you ask it is done" state of consciousness, the people perish. They are caught on the wheel of mortal illusion. They are always looking for a future reward, a future day of fulfillment. If it were ever to come, it would be *now*. So hark back to the words of the Master and begin the *Now*-ness of Life.

The Thing I Feared Has Come Upon Me
It has already come upon me, for it is within me. It is not something from which I can run away and hide. It is omnipresent as the air you breathe, but it exists *only* to you. The terror lying in wait to spring at you at the slightest suggestion, a jack-in-the-box which is released a thousand times a day, is all in you. Face the thing first within yourself and then the manifestation. "Stand and see the salvation of the Lord." Eventually, as you contemplate God in the midst of you, you begin to experience the love of God, and that does the trick, for "perfect love casts out fear." Now you are fearless, and "Jack" is back in the box of oblivion.

Patterns
All problems are merely patterns of congested thought superimposed on Wholeness. You have to

make up a problem by believing in a power opposed to God.

The answer already exists, and the moment you find it, you have no problem.

The Mr. A, Mr. B, and Mr. C of the old arithmetic days, having so many dollars, apples, or houses to sell, create a problem which does not exist, and the answer to this nonexistent problem is before the problem was self-imposed.

You superimpose the congested thought about yourself on your concept of God, and you then have a personal problem. The man next to you sees it as of no import—he knows the answer.

There is no reality to the problem except that given it by *you*. Thought is the substance and life of all evil, and as long as you keep thinking of a problem, it will remain.

Be absent from the body and present with the *Oneness*. Break the film of thought, and the picture it is holding into place will disintegrate. Change your position on the desert, and the mirage disappears.

"Come up higher," and the congested thought-picture does not exist and is not true.

Throw out the ballast of thought and move into a new level.

They Laughed Him to Scorn

"And they laughed him to scorn." They are speaking about Jesus. So much that he wanted to "tell" and so desirous was he of giving us the Law to

2 A.M.

these unspeakable things that he forgot their limitations, and so they *laughed him to scorn*. Can you hear those devastating shouts of laughter? So you can stop talking and begin showing.

"Many things I could not tell you in Jerusalem (but only for one reason) because of your unbelief." You just couldn't take them. What were they?

Man has worked out many inventions, many of them interesting but all of them temporal and subject to change without notice, and all of them merely trying to pattern the Divine.

Man was given dominion over everything—over, on, and under the earth, and even the elements—and when he finds this to be a state of consciousness, he can and will dispense with the inventions of man. Why not?

Resist Not

Against a backdrop of flaming, flaring life, comes Jesus. A whole army of picked legionnaires in their gold and scarlet dress and flashing swords become pastel and washed out against his gentleness, his nonresistance. "Thy gentleness has made thee great."

"Resist not evil, and it will flee from thee." Sometimes it is "resist not" and then is "resist evil"—and so "with all thy getting, get understanding." All these precious revelations are given to you to use at the precise moment they are needed. Ask Me and *I* will tell you.

Like Unto

The Presence is as tender music ... as a panoply of light ... as a mantle of soft feathers enfolding you ... as a cloud of exquisite perfume wafted from dew-drenched flowers at morn ... as feeding among the lilies ... as the pungent odor of pine trees in the rain ... as entering into those reaches where time is measured only by light-years ... as the zest that comes from entering into laughter.

Color

Your present degree of consciousness is the prism through which the invisible white Light of Jesus Christ is passed into manifestation. But It has to be put through the prism of *your* consciousness. Recognition that this is possible will cause some of these lovely colors of manifestation to appear. From celestial spaces, all these lovely experiences will come.

Nothing New Under the Sun

Listening to the modern radio with its commercials and its new discoveries, one is prone sometimes to imagine that the cliché "there is nothing new under the sun" has become a little outmoded. Yet this night, as I was browsing about among books on my table, I picked up a free translation of Ovid, Latin poet, born in 32 BC. He gives some Emily Post advice which sounds as if it might have been fresh copy from the editor's desk:

2 A.M.

> Let exercise your body brown;
> Don't slobber; see your teeth are clean,
> Your hair well cut and brushed right down;
> Your toga spotless, white and neat,
> Your sandals fitting to your feet.
>
> Remember too your nails to pare,
> And keep your armpits sweet beneath.
> Pluck from your nostrils every hair,
> With citron cure a noisome breath,
> And that is all you need to know.
> —Translated by F.A. Wright

Amazing, isn't it? Written years before the birth of Christ and yet with the same ideas rigidly adhered to at this date. You begin to see that the wheel of human thinking moves round and round, and we are bound to it until we awaken to the *inner consciousness* and free ourselves from the tedious picture of nothingness which apparently comes and goes, as the centuries of heavy human thought moves on.

How Should Evil

> How then should evil have reached me,
> when the arms of my Savior (inner Lord)
> held me to his breast.
> —Raimon Lull,
> Saint of Majorca, 12th century

This becoming conscious of the *oneness* of man and God through the Father-Consciousness eventually will take place in the struggling heart, and he will understand the nearness of it all and how it was that

Jesus went immediately to his Father—the Savior, the inner Power which is the point of contact between Spirit and matter; the place where the unseen becomes transmuted and changed, condensed, as it were, into the heavier substance called matter, or manifestation.

Once the sense of this oneness and nearness is recognized, new and wonderful capacities come into being. "Ways that ye know not of" are put into action. Evil conditions and beliefs flee before the recognition of this Presence as a *reality* and not as a power called into action by beseeching or begging; and eventually, the overtones of the lovely command "whatsoever you ask in my name (nature), that give I unto you." Man begins to sense this, to feel it, to discover a secret wellspring within, and to act from that elevation—to stand and see the salvation of the Lord.

Gradually, as the light of this Nearness becomes a reality to you, a radiance of It floods everything, and you begin to know with the ancient lamas that:

> Apart from one's own hallucinations, in reality there are no such things existing outside oneself as lord of death, or god, or demon, or the Bull-headed Spirit of Death. Act so as to recognize this.
> —*The Tibetan Book of the Dead*

The Alabaster Box

"Why was not the ointment sold for three hundred pence and the money given to the poor?" So the old question goes—give to charity and give to the poor, in spite of the Law, which says, definitely,

2 A.M.

"to the poor the gospel is preached," and the gospel is the "good spell," which will free the poor from the terrible bondage of poverty.

> There is indeed a Catholic doctrine of the *perpetual* virginity of Mary, the *birth* of Christ being no less miraculous than his incarnation: a doctrine that my first Spanish catechism expressed by saying that the Christ Jesus passed from his mother's bosom into her arms as a ray of sunlight passes through a pane of glass, without breaking it or staining it. This might properly be called "Virgin Birth."
> —George Santayana

Ambling Through Yesterdays

Pittacus, 615 BC, philosopher of Lesbos Island, thought that most men were bad. One time, when he was on a ship at sea which was overtaken by a terrible storm, the men began to shriek and pray to the gods. Pittacus shouted at them, "Keep quiet, you fools, or they will find out you are on board."

On another occasion, when someone questioned him as to what was piety, he remained silent. When questioned on why he remained silent, he replied, "I am silent because you are putting questions about things with which you have no concern."

During a certain threatened invasion, the inhabitants of the town were rushing to the sea, carrying their valuables, hoping to escape by ship. They passed Pittacus, empty-handed, and asked him why he didn't take his valuable things with him. He said, "I am taking the only valuable thing I have with me" and proceeded on his way empty-handed.

> "You cannot bend a stiff mind."
> "He that is fair is fair in appearance, but he that is good will soon seem fair also."
> "When anger rises in the breast, restrain the idly yelping tongue."
> "Do not meddle with the pebbles (sacred things).
> —Sappho (612-580 BC)

I Am Alpha and Omega

"I am Alpha and Omega." The Alpha is the appearing Jesus and the Omega is the Christ—the completion of the circle of life which causes the temple of God to appear in all its beauty and loveliness.

When the Christ (Soul) and Jesus (body) are united, then the mystic marriage takes place and Jesus Christ Consciousness takes place—the temple which could be apparently destroyed over and over yet remain intact.

You are the temple of the living God when this takes place and the direct operation of the God-power likewise takes place. So raising aloft this recognition, you find that you, the Jesus Christ Consciousness, are generator and progenitor of everything in your universe just as the man Jesus discovered and passed along to you. Everything that is coming to you is to

2 A.M.

be generated and recognized as existent within you. Everything you seek is already within the "darkened" temple of you ("I came a light," etc.), and so you begin to discover and find and stir up the gift of God that is already within you. Do you hear?

Breathless Adoration

And sometime or other, or perhaps many times, a space of breathless adoration will come to you — that suspended, golden moment when you are "there" — and at that time, many things will be impressed, told to you. As a great musician hears the entire symphony in a single note, so in this infinite second of pure recognition, you will see all and perceive all. At that moment, the bread is broken with you, and you behold the glory of it all.

The angel of His presence may brush you ever so lightly with his wings, and you will understand.

A new Song of Songs begins to unfold within you. A new day dawns, and you are "Still, still with thee, when purple morning breaketh." You are *there*.

And again the same angel of His presence might strongly enfold you with his wings in the noonday fury of life, when the passing maelstrom of thoughts and events is engulfing you to such an extent it is impossible to move. This infinite second of Light comes, and you are again breathless in adoration.

"Ou Sont Les Neiges D'antan?"
—Francois Villon

They Say

But "where are the snows of yesteryear?" Most of them have been incorporated into trees, plants, rivers, and oceans—all of them changed in form.

Where are the thousand and one lectures and words of Truth you heard in yesteryears? Those vital, burning words which awakened in you the warmth of true recognition, for the moment at least. They are submerged in the thick soil of the subconscious mind, lost to view and forgotten. Like the desert filled with seed of wonders to come, yet barren as to manifestation, so many of us have found it.

"I shall restore to you the years that the locust hath eaten" is as much a law as any other uttered by the Spirit. How will this restoration take place? What will happen? How the transformation, the transfiguration?

And then the prodigal remembered—not the fleeting, passing memory of the human thought, but the deep recognition of something that was a reality—the recognition of his divinity. The remembrance of all this fire which had been lighted years ago came to mind, and the new journey back to the Father-Consciousness began.

So as you begin to identify yourself with your *permanent* identity, it is like the drenching rains to the seed-filled desert. All the unseen, unheard contacts dropped into the ground, lo! these many years, begin to come to life. All the truth you have taken in becomes alive and moving. Like the mass of leaven

2 A.M.

leavening the whole mass of meal, so it is with this recognition of your Christ-Self.

The descent of the Holy Ghost awakens the slumbering ideas and truths you have been storing away for years, and every germ of good begins to unfold. A million forgotten words and laws spring into consciousness—the whole mass is leavened, and the "snows of yesteryear" are found in new and lovely manifestation.

Nothing has been lost.

Reaping

"But this I say, He that soweth sparingly shall also reap sparingly; and he which soweth bountifully shall reap bountifully."

If you are not getting enough of the substance for daily life, it is not because there is not plenty there but because you are sowing sparingly. Do not try to buy the truth. Do not give expecting to get returns but give from the love of God in your heart, and it shall return to you "pressed down and overflowing." "God is not mocked." Do not make a stock exchange of Him. He is a poor investment if you are doing it for returns.

Are you sowing sparingly? Have you taken your stance? God is not mocked. He that soweth bountifully shall reap bountifully. No matter if you have sown into those who have been dishonest and vicious—never mind. Everything you have given in Love will return unto you bountifully, no matter what liars, crooks, thieves, and false witnesses have eaten of the bounty of your giving. You cannot lose—it is impossible. This is a law of the fourth dimension. So look well to it all. How do you sow?

Receiving
"John (Love) answered and said, A man can receive nothing (not anything), except it be given him from heaven."

Well—what will you do with it? Are you still looking to a man to give you something? You will be mistaken and find yourself in the desert of waiting, never-ending waiting. Why don't you turn to this law of recognition and take your gift from God?

Love of God
"The Father (within you) loveth the Son (body-temple) and hath (already) given all things into his hand."

How's that? Can you believe with the simple, wonderful recognition of the Presence? Can you? He giveth all things into his hand. Is that wonderful?

Contemplate this for a moment. Are your hands empty? And if so, why?

Reversal
Hold this page up to the mirror and find it reversed. In the mirror of human thought, everything is reversed. "When I would do good, evil I do." Everything measured by the pattern of human

2 A.M.

thought is evil because it is seen from the reverse position of God.

Le Chef Extraordinaire

Did you ever think of Jesus as a chef? Well, at least he was a chef on one occasion. When the disciples had been working all night in the waters of dreary human chance and fate, he appeared to them and asked them, "Children, have you any meat?"

"No" was the reply. "We have fished all night and caught nothing."

Sounds just like the usual answer. "I have tried all the brands of metaphysics, paid (pardon me) through the nose, gone to practitioners, teachers, etc., etc., and I am weary."

Well, what are we going to do about it? There is not much one can do; the same old human pattern of destiny keeps right on. The human think-pattern cannot escape its "te deum" of nothingness and futility.

Don't go on talking about what you have done or left undone—wait a minute … you've admitted you have worked all night and gotten nothing. "Night" did you say? Yes, that's what I thought.

And now you are going into elaborate details of what you did or did not do in the dark.

Well, you couldn't see what you were doing anyway. Now that the Light is here, you are going to spend all this lovely illumination telling of your mistakes and how you fished and fished and fished and so and so and so!

You won't even listen to what is being said to you—or perhaps you will.

Well, children, "cast your nets on the right side." Simple, isn't it?

No, you have plenty to say about how you *know* you have been fishing in the same waters all night and gotten nothing; how you tried and tried and tried to make things go and have treated and treated and treated to make it "work." So you *know* there is nothing for you right where you are.

But maybe you will listen and finally obey the Consciousness within you, which says: right where you are *is* everything.

"Sounds like a lot of cheap metaphysics to me." Well, that's exactly what it is as long as you *try* to work it out by limited human thinking.

But perhaps you will stop this foolishness long enough to come under the glory of "believe," and then you will let down your nets on the *right* side of the boat.

Good heavens! (Pardon me.) You cannot draw them in, and then all of a sudden, like the disciples, you discover you are naked, and you go overboard because you are ashamed of your nakedness.

You ought to be ashamed when the hypocrisy of your protested faith is exposed. And I should think you would blush (I won't be so gauche as to say your face would be "red") when you see the very

2 A.M.

same old nets so filled with fish that you cannot draw them in.

Well goodness! What's a person to do? You're not going to do anything but be forgiven again—yes, seventy times seven—until you begin to really *believe* in Me.

And then you come ashore to find that Jesus has breakfast ready for you, and you sit down and eat and more than likely say, "It is wonderful. I didn't know Jesus could cook. Where in the world did he get the frying pan and the wherewithal to clean and prepare the fish for cooking, the wood, fire, etc?"

It is practically impossible for the old human "think tank" to produce any motion that could take in such a thing, let alone do it. But you did eat the meal, didn't you? And I suppose about the only thing we can say in closing is that Jesus was "automatically wonderful"—and so are you when you *let* that same mind be in you which was in him. What say?

Chapter XIV

Shadows

Since matter is the shadow of the Spirit (Spirit slowed down to a point of visibility), it likewise follows that matter and all manifestation is depending upon Spirit to sustain it. The moment the consciousness is withdrawn (the moment you let go of anything in consciousness), the manifestation begins to disintegrate and disappear. In fact, from the moment a thing appears in manifestation, it is on its way out. So if you only have a manifestation and no consciousness back of it, it will sooner or later disappear.

If you have a consciousness of substance, you will be able to cast infinite shadows of manifestation into the world of matter. If you have the *shadow* of substance (money), it will automatically melt away. The consciousness of substance can be manifested anywhere. If you have a consciousness of money, it may materialize in the coin of *any realm*. But if you only have a symbol, it is different—it is subject to loss, theft, or expenditure.

If you have a consciousness of substance, you can go to any country and cash in on it, or cast a shadow of it. If you have only money, it is different. Substance can never be counterfeited, but money can, etc.

2 A.M.

If you have a consciousness of locomotion, or of an automobile, it will materialize from time to time in various types of cars. But if you only have a "shadow" (a car), it is on its way out, and you will have to make another *demonstration* before you can have another.

Do you begin to see that every manifest thing is on its way out the moment it comes in? When you "loose it and let it go" in consciousness, the disintegration begins and carries on into the fullness of the Word. The man in authority was one who could call or dispatch manifestation. "When I say go, he goeth; and when I say come, he cometh." He was comparing himself with Jesus, who could call into manifestation *whatsoever* he would and could also dispatch the fig tree so that by sundown it was withered away.

As you walk in front of ten thousand mirrors, you cast, without doing a thing, ten thousand reflections, and you take them away without effort, for you are the reflector. The whole material universe is a maze of mirrors reflecting you and your consciousness. You are the man in authority, and pretty soon you will understand the difference between consciousness and thinking. You will begin to *see* with the single eye of Spirit and know why Jesus dared to send his disciples into expression without thought of the purse or the scrip, etc., knowing that the thought-taking process could produce nothing of worthwhile value. "Who by taking thought can add one cubit to his stature" or bring out an automobile or a house or, for that matter, a red hat?

When you can answer the question, "How does this man speak, seeing he has no learning?" then you will be able to differentiate between thinking and consciousness.

If you had been born blind and the Voice had said to you, "Will you receive your sight," certainly it would have done no good for you to think about sight, for you have never had any. It would appear, then, that you are forced to recognize a thing called *consciousness*. Either you take the impossible by consciousness or the possible by thought. So "choose ye this day whom you will serve."

"With all your getting, get understanding."

Five Bad Minutes

If you want to experience a really bad five minutes, just try to imagine what your life would be like without the name *Jesus Christ*. It is something so black and hopeless, only the way of the extrovert is left open. Without the name *Jesus Christ*, there would be no more going within to the Father or Christ. All your living would have to be out in the world of things. You would have to hew down a tree and make a god of it or melt your gold trinkets and cast an image. You would have to divert all the unseen power of God into the power of things and beliefs.

All the other people in the universe make no difference, no historical character but whom you

2 A.M.

could do without; but *this one* would make such a void and such a confusion and futility that it would seem like being in the menagerie of a big circus when the center pole fell down. The whole of creation would be down about your ears, and the roaring and howling of the *animal thing* would be terrifying enough.

More Snows of Yesteryears

Years and years and years ago, I remember my mother calling me to one side, when I had been bitterly criticizing another child, and saying to me:

"Son, God has spared you one very unpleasant duty—that of judging others."

And again, when I was flushed with the first discovery of God as *everywhere present* and I went to her and said, "But you see, Mother, God *is* here."

To which she replied, "Well, if you believe that He is here, why do you stress the word *is*?"

To which I replied, "Well, Mother, you just don't understand."

And so years and years and years after the soft blessing fell upon almost frozen ground, I am experiencing some of the truth of the early words—just beginning to *hear* them after all these years. The snows of yesterday are not lost—they are there, waiting transmutation into everyday *life*.

Houses

"And God said, the houses of the Egyptians (those who believe in anything else than Jesus Christ) shall be darkened, but the houses of the true believers shall be filled with light."

It isn't a matter of running along a street to see whether a house be lit with a million candlepower light or whether it be in darkness—it is the man you meet. You realize at once whether he is lighted with the recognition of the Immaculate Conception or whether he is still struggling in the Stygian darkness of other days.

There are Light houses and there are dark houses—you are meeting them daily. The word has already gone out. In the streets, shops, and market places, you come upon those houses. They are either lighted with the Word or they are in darkness of the present-day foolishness.

"Salute no (not any) man you pass on the highway of life." Flee from that man "whose breath is in his nostrils." What does a man who still wants to argue, compare, or discuss the truth know about it? So flee from that one.

If You Don't Know, You Just Don't Know

I knelt at the so-called tomb of Jesus and prayed. A "Christian" standing beside me said, "Do you believe in that?"

2 A.M.

I went up the sainted stairway in Rome on my knees. A "Christian" beside me said, "Well, of all the superstitious persons."

I showed some Hollywood party crashers who came to my home one night a lovely, life-sized Buddha and said to them, "If you burn a piece of incense and say a prayer, it will come true." They did—and went away telling the world that I was a worshiper of Buddha.

I burned a candle in a Catholic church, knelt, and prayed. A person said, "What?"

If you take nothing with you, nothing is there. If you do not understand, it doesn't matter.

Anyone who is healed at the Shrine of Lourdes takes with him the recognition of the Truth—and so if you don't see, you just don't—too bad. "When ye pray, believe that ye receive," and that is the Law. It is not according to the ideas of man.

If you do not know God, you cannot see Him in hell. That's where you need Him most—not in a church house.

The Kingdom of Heaven

Jesus insisted that this (right here and *now*) is the kingdom of heaven. Well, it looks like hell most of the time, and so there must be something in the degree of recognition which changes the appearance after we stop judging from appearances and judge righteous judgment. Is it going to be the *word* of

Jesus or *your* human findings? Make up your mind—and abide by it. Thank you.

What Is It You Want?

"Go in and possess the land." That is the only way you are going to get it. It isn't coming to you by a human miracle; it will only come when you go in and "possess" it. When you take a new state of consciousness (the land) as real and true and accept it as yours, then the miracle to the human sense will appear, and the "little ones" will say, "What a wonderful demonstration." But you will say, "Thank you, Father," Understand? Because you *believe*.

I Shall Give You the Keys

Can you take them? Keys to the mysteries. Do you believe? If you have nothing with which to take them, you cannot have them. If there is no chalice ready, no wine will pour. If there is no vessel, no oil can run. And these are not made ready in the hope they will be filled; they are made ready to receive the *recognized* substance, which is even now pouring into manifestation.

Know Ye Not That …

Ye men of Athens, "Know ye not that ye are gods?"

And Jesus said, "Call no man your Father, for one, which is in heaven, is your Father."

And the mother of Alexander the Great said to him, "You are not the child of the king, Philip, but

2 A.M.

are a son of the god Ammon." And he believed it and acted like it and showed such perfect dimensions of this power that he conquered the world before he was thirty and set a physical example before his men that would have been the envy of Praxiteles or a Phidias. So perfect was his body and mentality he automatically commanded attention and respect.

You may still be under the thought that Alexander was a heathen, a pagan, and believed in strange gods. I wonder how much stranger were his gods than those you subscribe to in the name of the *one* God. But nevertheless, by believing in his divinity, he was able to bring it through on all planes of existence. When he "asked" his Ammon god, he got results. Do you? And if not, why not? Perhaps it is because in your heart you still believe and subscribe to the teachings of the mortal mind, which says you were born of woman, are of few days, filled with trouble, etc.

Was Alexander, then, more divine than you? *It would seem so.* He accepted his power as something from God (his God was called Ammon) and acted accordingly. Anyone who can accept his God-heritage will discover a definite uptilt in his life and affairs.

Flee from the man "whose breath is in his nostrils," for he does not believe you were God-created but a product of physicality; and if this be the case, you have nothing but problem after problem to work out. If, however, you happen to take Jesus at his word and believe—even in so small a degree as a grain of mustard—you will begin to see some God-dimensions of power working in and through the confusion of human thought.

The Divine Bookkeeper
"I shall restore to you the years that the locusts have eaten."

There is a divine Bookkeeper, and "vengeance is mine" is His trademark—which means that the "statements" will be sent out at the proper time.

So turn over all your accounts to Him—all the money you have lost, all the money that has been "stolen" from you, all the bad accounts and mistakes—and presently you will find it all coming back with interest.

"Ten sheep for one" is the law. Stand and see the salvation of the Lord in matters where you have given and done in accordance with the law and then seemed to have been the dupe of an unscrupulous person, or where you have lost after following your highest urge. There is no discount in God.

It is all so wonderful. "Not one jot or tittle shall be released until the law be fulfilled."

You pass along ... presently some old account is returned, fully paid with interest. It is wonderful. Turn over everything to the Bookkeeper. Statements will be issued at the right time. You can lose nothing by doing good. "Vengeance is mine." *I* will take care of it.

2 A.M.

And If I Go ... (In answer to a sorrowing heart)

The autumn fires had been lighted by flaming sumac and maple. Nothing would quench this riot of color but the soft, white blanket of the first snow. Yonder at the edge of the world, purple, unspeakably vivid mountains cut sharp lines of unearthly beauty against azure skies. Here and there a group of black-green cypresses stood like sentinels, yet almost as if floating in the golden haze which hung cloyingly to the green valley.

It was one of those strange, weird moments in life when so much can happen—almost all can happen, and yet nothing takes place. And then it was that the Word came: "Yes, he will come again."

And suddenly, wading knee-deep in the golden mist, his helmet slipped back from his fair young brow; his hands signaling from the distance, he came. In a hushed moment, he parted the curtains, the veils so thin, and talked to me of wondrous, lovely things; talked to me for eons in a single moment. And in that moment, he showed me again, as did the Elder Brother, that he was and is flesh and blood and not a vaporous spirit; that the warm, sweet blood of him which had poured on some foreign field had taken nothing but had given him the right to bless the land with something so precious it was bound to change things there. *Something* would be better and holier for that baptism.

"And if I go, I will come again," whenever you believe in Me as a reality and not as a strange voice or vaporous manifestation, issuing from some dank, dark room or human imagination, but when you dare to *believe*—not in the lisping words of the babe, but the full diapason of Life.

"Thy son liveth." It is beyond speculation—it was established by Jesus. It is possible to any man. Selah!

I Sing of You

"Je chante de toi, et tu peut m'acceptez pour ton pretre." So sings Rostand. "I sing of thee, and you may accept me as your high priest."

Such a lovely idea. You are the temple of the living God through which all the wonderful things may pour. All the lovely and wonderful things you have seen in another—and yes, things that have never yet been expressed—must and will be expressed through you, *the temple of the living God*. Understand the word *living*—not something you start into expression through thought but through recognition. You are the temple.

I sing of thee, and you may accept me as your high priest. Isn't it wonderful when you consecrate your body and life to Me? None of the old monastic thing but just a *living*, straight into the kingdom of heaven. Can you take it and get over the limited thing called "John Smith"? Through you, the temple of the living God, comes this wonderful Light.

2 A.M.

I sing of thee, and you may accept me as your high priest. After that you may expect anything—I said *anything*.

I sing of thee, and you may accept me as your high priest.

Who by Taking Thought
"Who by taking thought can add one cubit to his stature?"

> Most midgets add several inches to their stature after passing 30, and not a few have actually grown out of the realm of midgetdom— which for most theatrical purposes stops at four feet, five inches. An extraordinary case is that of Eddie Wilmot of Minneapolis, who at 18 was a star performer in the Lilliputian troupe. After a severe illness, he began to grow again. Today at 28 he is over six feet tall. For some unknown reason, no midget ever becomes bald.

But the fact that it takes place, as evidenced by the above portion of an article by Robert W. Marks, *Variety Magazine*, is enough to make one pause a little when confronted with the so-called fixities of the human body.

Incurable diseases, malformations, and all these more or less fixed things are no more incurable when handled by consciousness than the height of the midget above referred to. Since matter is Spirit slowed down to a point of visibility, it can change its form and shape and assume perfect outlines when the right degree of consciousness of perfection is assumed.

"Then went he in and shut the door," and exactly what he told his Father, what he discovered as real and true, that—yes, that particular thing—was "called from the housetops" or, in other words, was made apparent to the man in the street. So don't be too sure that the apparently frozen atoms of your body cannot be thawed out, set in motion again, and assume the perfect picture shown to you on the mount. If you are not a midget mentally, you will not be a midget otherwise.

Feeling

You shall find Me when you *feel* after Me. Where am I going to feel? In the think-mind or heart?

Why do you pursue the study of Truth? Have you hypnotized yourself into believing that you believe? Do you believe, or are you still wanting to make some demonstrations or manifestations? Do you *believe*? Because if you do, you have signs, plenty of them.

One Moment Please—Answer This One

After Jesus had fed five thousand from two fishes and five loaves, they were instructed to pick up the pieces, and they gathered up twelve baskets full. Where did the baskets come from? Quite sizable to hold the scraps from five thousand people. Think

2 A.M.

about it, and you have a second miracle almost as big as the first.

Who was the man at the other gate? We only have one tiny verse about him. He was doing the same works as Jesus and speaking the same words.

It couldn't have been that the disciples reporting this could have stepped up their consciousness and were able to hear the selfsame Jesus talking to a group of more enlightened people—or could it? Giving them more enlightened food for consciousness, in the same fourth-dimensional Jerusalem. I think it could have been and was. The moment you are ready, the Master will appear. "My sheep hear my voice." Can you *hear* me?

Other Side of the Lake

If you get pressed too much by human thinking, you can "go over to the other side of the lake"—that is, if you can.

All these wonderful laws are given to you if you can take them, but you cannot *try* to take them. Do you see?

Also, you can pass through the cloud of human thoughts and thought-pictures. Every sharp elbow will move out of your ongoing if you will *go*. You can pass through any cloud of human manifestation if you *can*.

It is no use trying to make a person into a vegetarian as long as he has a desire for meat. No matter what he thinks about it being good for him or right or the only way, it will amount to nothing, and the very vegetables that help others so much will seem to harm him.

No use taking up Truth because you think it is right and want to believe, as long as you know evil and human thought is the only truth. Just won't work, for sooner or later you will rush back to your first love, and all your efforts and straining will be for naught—may even work evil in your human-thought world.

The Meek Shall Inherit the Earth

Dumb as an ox ... don't know a thing ... not clamoring with the outside ... just as meek as can be.

Listening and listening and listening and not saying a word—and then the head man comes along amidst all the raucous contestants and says, "Thaddeus, you come down out of that tree. I am going to have dinner with you today."

Well, for heaven sakes—I thought that "loud speaker" was going to get the prize, but they gave it to that funny little old thing who was as meek as anything and as dumb as an ox.

Well, goodness—what's a person going to do?

On Being Allergic

We pass through one phase after another of human belief. Once it was Coué [developer of auto-suggestion], then it was sauerkraut juice, and then it was "my husband or my wife." And then it was that

2 A.M.

you were allergic to everything, so that a tomato could make your body shake like a quaking aspen, and you "just could not stand calling cards edged in purple." And who was to save your "precious darling from the flames"?

Well, a lot of people tried to, some at a pretty big fee, but presently your overripe personality made even the doctor allergic to you, and at last you discovered the awful truth that you were "allergic to yourself"—which is a rather grand way of saying you were utterly fed up with yourself. A good state to find yourself in, when you begin to see that you are allergic (or in the popular vernacular, poison) to everybody else, yourself included, for you may bestir yourself and awaken from your bemused state of living with your selfish self. You then find out that there is infinite wisdom in the words of Jesus: "Be absent from the body and present with the Lord."

Such a pleasant sensation to get away from that awful thing called "yourself" and to get acquainted with your Self. Try it the next time you feel allergic.

Chapter XV

So You Won't Talk?

So you won't talk? Well, then, you can take a city (new state of consciousness). Not so bad for holding your tongue. Pretty sure of results, too, for "the power of life and death are in the tongue." Sounds ominous, doesn't it?

"Keep silent before me." Why?

"Well, you see, my problem is ..." and then a Niagara Falls of evil and negativity bursts forth, all of which you immediately proclaim as false and untrue. But you have just set it into motion and have gotten the agreement of another on the same subject.

No one is spiritual enough for you to expose your evil mind to. When you merge into the light of the Christ-Consciousness, it will dissipate the darkness without having to put it through the human mind. So hold your tongue and take a city—a new state of consciousness.

"See that you tell no man." Show John.

If you are talking about your little self all the while, and your problem, you cannot hear what *I* have to say to the churches (your body), and so things in the church are not going to go right—too many dove sellers and money changers; no place for the Christ to come in.

2 A.M.

Don't you dare tell it. Keep every valve of your mind shut up, and presently the power of the risen Lord in the midst of you will break the pattern of the limited consciousness and come out into being. It is wonderful! Such a glorious experience is waiting for you.

I don't have to call you a fool again, do I? "Thou fool, do you not know that a seed must first fall into the ground and rot before it shall be made alive?" An acorn may contain a potential oak tree, but it has first to lose the shape of the acorn before it can take on the new shape of the oak tree. And that is about the thing that has to happen to you—you cannot have what the oak tree has coming to it as long as you are an acorn.

Secrecy helps mightily in bringing out this new stage of things. So don't talk. Evil will die if not spoken of. It lives on thought and agreement. And Truth will enlarge the borders of your tent until It has changed the whole face of things. Hold your tongue and take a city.

Not That Which Goeth In

"Not that which goeth in, but that which cometh out makes or defiles a man." It isn't what goes into your mind but what comes out after it has gone in. To be able to *see* a thing for what it is worth and dismiss it is to free yourself from ugly experiences.

The experiences in a dream are soon cast aside once you are awake. Nothing more than a disturbed memory of a bad dream takes place the morning after a nightmare. And so man finally begins to handle yesterday's bad dream or ugly pictures in the same light.

I Am the Truth

Henceforth, stop *using* the truth, exchanging this old, worn-out, profitless habit for the wisdom, "I am the truth." From that elevation of consciousness, everything you say or do is automatically blessed. So is it also with the Light. I do not use It—"I am the light." There is a vast difference in the results that will follow. And of course, "I am the way." I do not demonstrate it any more.

If you contemplate the difference in "knowing the truth" and "being the Truth," you will see the distinct advantage of this.

By reason of the precious revelation of Jesus Christ, "I am the truth," etc., do you see that all the impersonal qualities of God can be embodied and become personal. Hence, instead of using Love, you *are* Love. "I AM THAT I AM." What I AM? I am Love, Truth, Light, and with each acceptance, it comes into manifestation automatically in accordance with the degree of your recognition.

What power, then, is yours when you go into expression as the embodiment of Life instead of the bringer of health, and "having done all, stand and see." You have done all when you are the embodiment of the power instead of using it.

2 A.M.

When you glimpse the facts of Being and go in and posses the consciousness of the Presence, then you can truly "go into all the world."

You cannot possibly raise the dead unless you are the embodied Life eternal, nor can you heal the sick unless you are Life instead of "health" — which, after all, is the human concept of Life.

A little contemplation of this wonderful revelation will cause you to achieve that which you desire. You are the power in action, and the never-ending source of this power pours through, as the oil poured from the three drops and continued to pour until everything empty was full.

You can "go" and you can accomplish with the nonchalance and the divine indifference which Jesus expressed because of this established consciousness of being the idea embodied. "I AM THAT I AM has sent me into expression," and the limited human thought and power are absorbed into a great tower of Light.

Gradually we are beginning to see how it is that "all things are possible" — if you believe.

Are You at Home?

Browsing about in some ancient Latin translations, I found this "Terrific Honesty." The date is 200 BC. The participants in this "Terrific Honesty" are Ennius, early Latin writer and philosopher, and Scipio, also an early writer. Ennius went to see Scipio and was received by the maid, who said, "He is not in."

Ennius went on his way, knowing full well that Scipio was at home.

The next evening, Scipio went to visit Ennius. Ennius looked out from an upper room and called, "Not in."

"But," said Scipio, "you are in."

To which Ennius replied, "Listen—last night at your house, I believed your maid when she said, 'Not in.' Why in heaven's name cannot you believe me when I speak for myself?"

All diplomacy is deception, saying one thing and meaning another. You can mock everything but God—and He (the universal balancer and record keeper of you) cannot be mocked. So stop trying.

The other man might be fooled for a moment, but "I am not mocked" will take care of the final accounting. When you move with the current of the river, you flow into the universal Sea of Life. Otherwise, you are cast into the slough of appearances.

If you haven't enough money, health, or happiness, it is because you are not true enough. Sorry!

My Robe

Beliefs have been described as the graveclothes which Jesus laid aside when he resurrected himself. Woven in flimsy or intricate, heavy patterns, these must sooner or later be laid aside. The weight of these beliefs becomes too heavy unless they are transmuted into garments of Light and praise.

2 A.M.

"They cast lots for my robe." The robe for which men cast lots and are still casting lots is the *consciousness of Jesus Christ*—which is bid on by a thousand merchants of truth and sold out a thread at a time. It is not unlike the "splinters of the Cross" that one finds for sale in Jerusalem. If they were all assembled in one cross, it would be several miles high. Yes, they cast lots for my robe, but they cannot buy or sell My consciousness, for *I* am not there. *I* am over here—on the other side of the lake.

650 BC

> The fairest thing in all the world,
> some say, is a company of horsemen;
> And some, a regiment of marching soldiers,
> And some again, a fleet of ships;
> But I say the fairest thing is "the Beloved."
> —Sappho

More Robes
Since they found the graveclothes of Jesus in the tomb, the head cloths in a separate pile to one side, did Jesus go from the tomb naked or clothed? When you begin to really "see," there are miracles all over the place.

Resurrection
Perhaps you are prone to think only of Jesus as having resurrected? But before he did this, it is recorded that at the moment of his Crucifixion a

great earthquake (something that rent old, fast, hard, human thought patterns) took place, and graves were opened and saints arose and were resurrected. How many? No recording; perhaps hundreds or perhaps a few—but enough to cause you to know that resurrection is not confined to Jesus alone.

Easter

Easter is the logical New Year, for it is the time you start all over with a new embodiment—a thing or degree of consciousness which says, "Touch me not," to the former rubbish and human thinking of evil which had wound you about in the graveclothes of failure and laid you to rest. All this lovely symbology becomes real when you enter in as the actor in life instead of the spectator. "Go thou and do likewise"—enter into the play of Life. "Take up your cross … follow me." All these call for embodiment of action on your part. When are you going to drop the role of spectator and enter in and be saved?

Easter Morn

It was Easter morn. Soft, silver-gray streamers of light began reaching through the dark mantle of night, when the great discovery was made: "He is risen." And the eternal *present* tense of the verb makes it just as real today as then.

Someone has rolled the stone away from the tomb, and he is risen. At last he has resurrected himself—he has fulfilled the law: "I have power to

2 A.M.

pick it up and lay it down." At last he has brought it out of the tomb of his own creating.

From the time he is a baby, man starts building his own tomb. He runs through a thousand and one evil beliefs of childhood. His life is filled with *don'ts* and ways and means of protecting himself from the omnipotent evil of the world. All the time, he is laying stone upon stone in his tomb, and finally, when the world of human belief has crucified him, he is laid to rest, and history (his story) records that he died, was crucified.

Until he resurrects himself, he is going to stay there, and after he has arrived at this state, nothing on the outside can be done for him. It is either self-resurrection or nothing.

This Easter symbology is performed in a thousand and one degrees, although it is given to use in what would be the utterly impossible, that of self-resurrection from actual physical death. But there may be a thousand little deaths in your life when you discover that you are literally in a tomb of the impossible and where you recognize there is no help. When finally you *remember* your immortality, your permanent identity, and begin to pick it (your body) up and bring it out into the new world of "he is risen"—risen into a degree of consciousness above the former thing and you are "not there" in that place anymore—it is wonderful how you leave the graveclothes there and are clothed in the new raiment of Light.

So You Won't Talk?

Virgin Mary

No, I do not worship the Virgin Mary—I do not believe in idols. Yet in a strange and wonderful way, you do have to worship the Virgin Mary, for nothing new and wonderful is coming through you until you see that in order to release the new *impossible* picture, you must have a virginal mind, a clean sheet of paper upon which is impressed the desire of your heart. The virgin mind was overshadowed by the Father and conceived and brought forth. So the virgin mind, that state of consciousness which can *believe*, is ready for the immaculate conception to take place and later for the child to be born.

You cannot take a picture on an already exposed camera plate, and if you do, you get only confusion and chaos. Neither can you superimpose this new and beautiful revelation on the evil-filled human mind.

Come up higher. You profess to believe with your lips—do you begin to *see* the new degrees of recognition of the established thing? "Look again, the fields are white" is quite a reach past the human thought of "four months," but that stretch or reach can and will be made through recognition. So after all, you do worship the Virgin Mary consciousness.

My Word

> "But the anointing which ye have received (already) abideth in you, and ye need not that any man teach you, but as the same anointing

2 A.M.

> teachest ye all things, and is truth, and is no lie, and even as it hath taught you, ye shall abide in him."

You see, then, that the inspiration of your inner Lord will not only teach you but shall "lead you into all truth." It is so written in the Law. Who, then, can teach you? And when will you rely upon the inner vision of your Lord? You have already received the anointing. Do you believe? Do you seek the help of another? Do you still go a-whoring after false teachers, or will you accept the revelation of your own inner Lord? Am *I* he that should come, or look ye for another? Lean not on a broken reed but lean on Me. Where is the Me—and when are you going to believe in Me?

Light

> "Again, a new commandment I write unto you, which thing is true in him and in you: because the darkness is past (do you hear?) and the true light now shineth."

"He that hath ears, let him hear what the Spirit saith unto the churches (bodies/temples)." Do you hear? Do you believe? It saith, "and the true light now shineth." Does it? If not, why? And when are you going to "let there be light" take place in you? *Let* there be light—don't make it.

Concerning Teachers

"But whoso keepeth his word, in him is the love of God perfected; hereby know we that we are in him."

The increased importance of keeping the *word* is brought out. If your word is no good, you can expect the word of every other man to fail.

"My words are spirit and they are truth," and "they shall not return unto me void, but shall accomplish that whereunto they are sent."

The rich reward of suddenly coming upon this spiritual law of keeping your word is the love of God being perfected in you. Think what this might mean—the love of God, the thing that never faileth, *never faileth*. That is good enough for me—a law that never faileth. So look to your *word*—remembering that the human mind is "a liar and the father of it."

Yea, Yea and Nay, Nay

You either accept the thing that is presented to you or you do not. If you accept appearances and fail to "judge not from appearances but judge righteous judgment," then can you expect the results of your "yea" and "nay." The moment a picture is presented to you, you must have a "yea" or a "nay" for it. Watch—either "Yea, yea" or "Nay, nay." Watch.

The Carpenter

Jesus was the carpenter, Christ the indwelling Father. The blending of these two produced Jesus

2 A.M.

Christ, the Consciousness which could and did step down into visibility the unseen, finished kingdom of God. Without this point of manifestation, how could the stream of loaves and fishes, wine, gold, health, etc., come into manifestation?

The Jesus Christ Consciousness is possible to every man who professes *in his heart* that God has come in the flesh. The more constant the recognition of this "flesh" wherein you *see* God, the more effortless and unlabored is the flow of the unseen substance into manifestation.

"Let that mind be in you ... ." A thing that is to be *let* must be *possible*, but only when recognized; and when the understanding of Jesus Christ Consciousness is attained, even as a grain of mustard, you will begin to experience living in the temple of the living God, and your body-temple will be operated by the fatigueless Light and no more by the thing called health, which is circumscribed within the narrow confines of human thought.

"Stir up the gift of God that is within you." How can you do this until you recognize that such a thing is true, and how can you stir up a gift unless you know what the gift is?

"I shall arise and go to my Father" is only another way of showing how it was that the Jesus part of us (called by your personal name) eventually "remembers" something and goes straight to the Father and blends with Him, changing the substance, even as the leaven changes the meal. This changed

So You Won't Talk?

substance contacts both the visible and the invisible world and passes through its temple the Light which becomes the *bread from heaven*.

It is so wonderful when you see this, for the Light has then been set that is going to lead all men into salvation. Your Light will draw everything unto you. Presently you will experience this light of the Jesus Christ Consciousness and will know. Yes, you will see the Light of another "a long way off" and there, too, you will pass by many darkened houses. Without Jesus Christ, all is darkness.

Invocation

> "Stab my spirit wide awake."
> —Robert Louis Stevenson

There is that moment, too, when you "invoke" the Power, when the sheer feel of the Presence is so real to you that you can touch Me and "feel after" Me." Then is the Spirit in you awake, stabbed by the rays of revelation descending directly from the Godhead into the Soul of you. Lo and behold, it is wonderful!

Warning: Be sure you do not *try* to let.

Remember: Today is the only day—you are going to live today.

Also remember: When you enter Jerusalem (the new dimension), choose a colt upon which no man has sat.

2 A.M.

Jesus commanded his disciples to bring him a colt "whereon never man has sat." You are to enter your kingdom not by the teachings of another or on the skirts of another, but on a colt—a new, original concept of the Truth, upon which no person or personal teaching has been saddled.

Get away from persons, organizations, and things and discover *the way* within yourself, and when you have, you will begin for the first time to appreciate persons, organizations, and things for what they are—many of them glorious channels for light and revelation. But just the same, go into Jerusalem on a colt whereon no man has sat. So said one of my listeners.

The Voice

"I am the voice of one crying in the wilderness."

Could you hear a voice from the wilderness of human thought? And would you believe it if you did?

"My sheep hear my voice." If you cannot hear the voice of God when it speaks from the wilderness, how will you hear it when it speaks from heaven? If you cannot accept the promises of God, no matter through *what* source or temple they come, you cannot experience the delight of the New Day.

God's promises are kept. Man's promises are broken. So "what went ye out for to see, a man arrayed in purple and fine linen?" When you go out to hear the Voice and *obey* that Voice, no matter how the man is dressed, then the temple of God is with man, and when you begin to realize this, you will *hear* the voice of God speaking to you. Hence, a poor man could make you rich, even though he could not prosper himself, for any *temple,* or manifestation, can be used by God to speak to you when you are at the listening post of recognition.

Can you take it? Or do you want to argue about the temple (body) through which the Voice comes?

Call upon Me, and *I* will answer you (not maybe or perhaps), but can you hear Me, disregarding the temple through which the voice comes? *I* could speak to you through the burning bush, that is, if you could take it.

So a poor man may bring to you the *confirmation* of your affirmation, but your human intellect might block the manifestation because it would argue how impossible it was for that man to fulfill your wish. Nothing is said about that taking place—it is just the *confirmation.* When you receive a wire by Western Union that a fortune has been left you, you do not argue about Western Union giving you the money, though it is the channel through which you receive the news.

In other words, can you hear Me, or are you looking at the rags and tatters or the purple and fine linen?

"My sheep hear my voice"—not human words, but *My voice.*

2 A.M.

If the desert is to blossom as a rose, you are going to have to hear something which is obviously not true and is *impossible*. Can you take the promises and the confirmation that are to come through you as a result of your recognition of Me?

"Behold, I stand at the door and knock, and if any man hear my voice ... ." Can you open the door of absolute receptivity and *let* the manifestation in by accepting the promise and Word, irrespective of the temple?

Meditations

Yonder in the west, a lovely billowy cloud rested atop a purple mountain. A Cerulean sky made it look like a golden Viking ship coming into port. It was a lovely poem, so far beyond the reach of me, and yet I realized suddenly that lovely, evanescent cloud could be condensed into rain and finally frozen into ice cubes in the Frigidaire.

So it is with Spirit. The invisible is brought down to a point of visibility—the unseen becomes the seen. The void of longing, already filled with the All, becomes suddenly complete. Recognition of the Presence and the "way ye know not of" causes the *impossible* to take place. When it is understood, it will be a perfectly natural action of Spirit. Through the temple of man (the body), must all the mechanics take place. Until man believes in Jesus and his teachings about the temple (body), he will be hoping for a miracle or demonstration.

So You Won't Talk?

Jesus did everything through his body (temple). His references are well known: "Destroy this temple … ." "I have power to pick it up … ." etc.

With his own beautiful hands did he break the bread to increase, his lovely slim fingers of consciousness reaching up into the *invisible* source of the All and drawing from that source the thing "hoped for"—tangible evidence of things not seen.

So as your temple (body) is cleansed of the thought-taking evil, you will find new and more wonderful capacities within to bring into visibility the unseen. It will be natural and normal, not mysterious and fantastic. The "way ye know not of" is the way of stepping Spirit down to a point of visibility and changing its name to—*matter*.

Consciousness Versus Thought

"Who by taking thought … ." "I come at a moment you think not." All evil proceeds from human thought and is sustained by it. It is a liar and the father of it. It judges from appearances, and not one of its senses is capable of true judgment.

When the human mind is told about a person, it immediately constructs an image of him in its mind. It adds to and takes from and enjoys what it thinks is a good picture of the man. When it comes in contact with the man, it discovers that almost everything it had conceived or thought about the man is entirely false. What becomes of the image it had built by thought? In an instant, it disintegrates, and the *consciousness* of the man begins to appear.

The more you stay in the presence of the man the more the consciousness of him becomes established. From consciousness flows the stream of Light-thought, which has a basis upon which to rest—it never creates or adds to. A deeper consciousness of the man causes more Light-thought to flow forth.

So it is with the Christ. Becoming conscious of your divinity, you begin to lose the false pictures of yourself—the temple of the living God begins to change, and whereas, before you were blind, now you see without effort or strain.

Anything in consciousness takes place automatically and without the aid of human thought. Light-thought proceeds from consciousness, stands immovable on its basis.

Angels

Angels are not personalities but great centers of power and force—in other words, manifestations of the power of God stepped down to a point of visibility, great armies of reserve power which are at the command of the consciousness which has accepted its divinity as the Christ within. "Think ye not that I could call upon my Father, and he would send me twelve legions of angels?" "The works that I do, ye shall do also, and greater ... ."

When you call for the twelve legions of angels, they will appear and will, like the genie of the lamp, go into action, silently and invisibly, and will disintegrate the congealed thought-forces which are outpicturing such insurmountable proof of the power of evil. Nothing can withstand this invisible Power set into motion by your recognition.

Echo

When the conditions are right, the echo is there, and without effort it answers automatically. Can you "ask," knowing that the answer (echo) is already there, only awaiting releasement?

Before you ask, *I* will answer. The echo is already there the moment you set it in motion.

When you pray, believe that you receive. Keep your human thought away from it all, and you will have the *echo,* or answer, because it cannot help coming into being. Keep your thought out of the picture.

Adultery

If it is given to the child, surely you have a chance. When you stop committing adultery with everything spiritual, you will see it appear. The business of the adult human mind is to commit adultery automatically. When it would do good, it does evil because of its thought-taking propensity. The childlike mind or consciousness is open to take

2 A.M.

the impossible—to accept, to recognize, to possess. Stop committing adultery.

A New Word I Give unto You

Many of the hackneyed, overworked words of metaphysics are falling into the dust. They are so worn-out; all of the meaning has drained out of them.

Recently, in looking over some words, I wondered why we had hung on to the word *problem*. Webster Unabridged gives this meaning:

> Problem: A perplexing question, situation, or person. A matter involving difficulty in solving, settling, or handling, (as to solve a problem of how to prevent war).

Looks pretty hopeless and negative. But we are through with negatives and denials and have entered into the New Dimension. We do not try to *work out* health. If we follow the revelation of Jesus, we start with the "it is done" state and travel back through the congested human thought-pictures, disintegrating them and revealing the finished thing or project. So why not establish the new word—that you have a *project* to reveal instead of a *problem* to work out?

According to Webster, we have the definition:

> Project: To externalize any objective. To cast the transmitting agent into the crucible and thereby bring out precious substances. To cause to fall into space.

So You Won't Talk?

Any one of these is enough to give you the upgush of Life, which will *project* the project you have in mind.

Now then, let us look to our project and let the *problem* fall into the grave—uncoffined, unknelled, and unsung.

Speak English?
    "Speak English?"
    "Yes, can you understand it?"

Without straining, trying, working, knowing the truth, without emotionalism or excitement, you automatically reply, "Yes"—and automatically ask at the same moment, "Can you understand me?"
    "Master, will you heal me?"
    "Yes, can you accept it?"

And without effort, Jesus healed, raised the dead, etc., etc. From the standpoint of Consciousness, manifestation automatically flows into being. It is effortless and natural. Without "taking thought" or trying to make something unnatural or impossible happen, the recognition of any degree of Life will produce in like kind its fruits or manifestation.

"Who touched me? ... for I perceive that virtue went out of me."

Who spoke to me? For I perceived that English went out from me. It is impossible to withhold manifestation when you touch the Consciousness.

Thinking you can speak English inhibits you at best. It is difficult to speak when you constantly

2 A.M.

have to think about it—about your words, letters, and phrases. It is an effort, and if you manage to get out a few sentences, you imagine you have worked a miracle. And you *have*, from that level of consciousness.

"Come up higher." You come up higher by being still and knowing that I AM (in midst of you) is God—by recognizing your own divinity, the Father within as a point where God can and does flow through into manifestation easily, naturally, unemotionally—automatically. It cannot be otherwise.

Point of Attack

Remember the old conundrum, "If a man threw a stone at you, would you attack the man or the stone?" If an evil thought picked a man up and threw him at you, would you attack the man or the thought?"

Your decision would determine just what the outcome would be. As long as the war-thought continues without being corrected, it will throw nation against nation, and no matter how many millions of soldiers are uselessly mown down, the idea will flourish and reproduce itself again and again, until the thought which is causing it is eradicated.

It is of little use to smear on a hand lotion to get rid of a blood disease. Don't attack the lack of money in your life. It is the thought back of it that needs correction or eradication.

When After

Always, after you have run hither and yon and you have been defeated and disheartened, do you turn unto Me and find rest for your soul. *I* have asked you to call upon Me … ask of Me … seek Me … lean upon Me. But not until you have tried everything else have you come to Me. Why?

Man's extremity being God's opportunity, give to Me this opportunity. Relax, call, ask, seek, lean on Me, and find rest.

Vision

I have not the extension of vision sufficient to see any miracle until that miracle takes place in me—and then I see it everywhere, and it is quite natural. When you are lifted up to a new state of consciousness, you appropriate and take, as natural and true, everything that is manifest on that plane. When you enter a warm room, your body, though almost frozen, automatically takes on the temperature of the room. No effort—it must take place. So in whatever city you enter (whatsoever state of consciousness), you immediately appropriate all that it has to offer as natural and true.

What You Take

First perform the thing within your consciousness—in the unseen, call it finished and done. "My Father (permanent Identity) worketh hitherto, and I (the body of Jesus) work." And when my Father, the

2 A.M.

permanent Identity, does the work, the Jesus (the John Smith of you), carries out the mechanics. The whole machinery is set in motion by this recognition, and the invisibility is stepped down to a point of visibility.

"Before you ask, I will answer." There are no questions in God and no problems. Man is the one who introduces these things—and then, being so bemused, he starts trying to "make" an answer or to "work out" something. It is hard for him to start with the answer and dissolve the problem or question he has superimposed on Life. But that is the way Jesus did it.

Why not do a right-about and go within and finish with it. What you tell Me (the Father, your permanent Identity), that shall (not maybe or perhaps) be "called from the housetops." Do you begin to see how it is that what you *take* you can *have*—and only that?

Time

"A thousand years are as a day; a day is as a thousand years." Time is only the distance between two events in human thought. It is always *now* in consciousness. You have, then, all the time needed for the slow human thinking to get its work done, and you can also telescope the thing until you can "look again" and the fields will be "white with harvest." You telescope and elongate the human thing called *time* to suit your purpose. It is one of your capacities—a gift of the Christ-Mind. Do you believe?

The Gesture

You must make the gesture. "Rise and walk" is only made manifest at the instant you make the gesture of rising. "Open your eyes" can only give the fulfillment of sight when you make the gesture. So after the stage is set and the child is ready to be born, there is a final gesture—the final delivery. Sometimes it is instantaneous, but it is always there.

"Thrust in the sickle and reap." Sounds like a pretty big effort, but everything you do in the Christ-Consciousness is going to seem like a Herculean task until you "make the gesture," and then you discover it is nothing. The moment you enter into a consciousness, you discover you have *always* been there, for the *former things*, thoughts and beliefs, are passed away; they shall not come into mind or be remembered anymore.

Finding Him

Oh, that I might find Him. Well, you're never going to until you look for Him in the only place He exists: in your consciousness.

When you do this, you find Him in everybody and everything. What you accept for yourself as finished and done, as consummated, can be fulfilled through any *temple*. Do you see this? You are the one

2 A.M.

who sets it in motion by your recognition that *it is already done*.

"I thank you, Father—I knew this was done," etc., and it was done—and it *did* embody. So begin with the answer before the question since the answer does exist before the question, and this recognition will release the manifestation, or give it a body.

Chapter XVI

From an Old London Note Book

Thumbing through an old notebook, I found these two lovely poems, which came through in a class of self-expression:

The Chalice

Dust—drought—and heat.
As far as eye could reach,
A sense of desolation and despair.
No shade—no rest—a throbbing ache of pain;
A weary stumbling on, with burning feet,
Across the parched and sandy wastes alone.

And then—a memory of restful shade,
Of living waters gushing from the depths
Of ancient wells that once I used to know.

I closed my eyes, to hold the vision there,
And stumbled back, by half-forgotten ways,
Until, within the shimmering haze, appeared
A mighty rock, and in its cool gray shade
The ancient Fount still poured its treasures forth,
Sparkling and clear.

A throng of travelers pressed
Close to the water's edge, and at their feet
Were vessels—some of pearl, of beaten gold,
Of hand-wrought silver, and a few of clay
From village potters' wheels.

2 A.M.

I stooped to drink,
When from the clamoring crowd
A voice cried: "Stay!
The cup thou hast is not of good design;
See! Here is one of workmanship more rare;
'Tis jeweled, too, and finer far than thine."
"Nay," cried another, "he knows naught at all.
This one holds more. Come, stranger,
Drink of mine."

I paused. A tortured memory returned
Of sunbaked plains, and stifling,
Thirst-filled nights,
Of fruitless wanderings in a barren land.
Should I delay for futile argument?

I seized a cup; and, kneeling in the sand, I drank.
And, as my thirsting spirit found
Healing and Life, with eager hands again
I raised my vessel to that Fountain old;
And lo! to me, the chalice was pure gold.

—Elizabeth Challyn

Recognition
(To W.C.L. in recognition)

Supernal I!—so long imprisoned by
This blindfold tyrant Me!
I know thee now; and knowing do not dwell
On the black years I held thee
Pent in the abysmal dungeon of my will,
Unrecognized, unseen, as through
My darkened universe I blundered,
Hot with strife, to seize and clutch my own.

This ever mocked me, slipped my grasp;
Or, if attained, left me unsated still;
The apples of Hesperides were dust,

And made me thirst the more; while thou,
The only one my spirit craved,
Lay, a forgotten captive, bound and chained
Within the deep recess of my being,
Waiting to give me all.

But now I see! I know thee for myself,
The God of me: and from thy
Native loveliness I strike the chains
Forged by my ignorance
And cry with joy,
"All hail, thou winged one, I let thee free!
Arise, come forth and shine,
Thou I of me!"
—G. Marion Burton

The Wanderer
(The Mood)

Dedicated to Walter Lanyon
in deepest gratitude.

Wayfarer … vagabond … wanderer, I,
Over the trails of the earth and the sky!
And if I tarry, or if I go,
I cannot tell you … I do not know!

Maybe, tomorrow, I'll spread out my wings,
Soar with the lark as it joyously sings!
Breast the west wind, to the rim of the world!
Find where the dawn's crimson banners are furled!

Nay, do not follow me!
Maybe quite soon I'll spy out a moon,
Where it's drenched in the sea …
Bathe in its silver, in bright rhapsody!
Shining, and argent, and free!

Or, maybe, I'll wander the sun-lighted fields;
Lay me down deep in the grasses and weeds,

2 A.M.

Piping my reeds!

Yesterday found me within the green wood,
Brushed by green branches
And sun-dappled leaves!
Then, of a sudden, all breathless I stood;
There at my feet was his bright pattern,
Breathless, I heard him—wild Pan!

I traced his hoof-marks to where his trail leads,
Piped on his syrinx and blew on his reeds!
And then caught a bluebird and rode on his wing,
I who am wayward ... and wandering!

Ah, do not follow me ... I do not heed
All of your blandishments! Only your need
Stops me ... and draws me ... and binds me to you!
Only your need drowns out wild Pan and his reed!

Nay, do not follow me, lacking the might
To chart straight your flight!
For I shall part the curtains of the night,
And I'll swing upwards till all memory blurs;
And then, on upwards, to incalculable height
Of distant "Betelgeuse!"
And perched upon her frigid, jagged edge,
I'll peer far down from this sapphire ledge,
To learn the alchemy of that blue light that's hers!

And there among the swinging, paling stars,
Remote from Earth, at this illimitable height,
I'll watch the golden chariot of the sun
Climbing the shadowy mountains of the night!

And when shall I return? Who knows? Who sees?
No human praise, or blame, shall draw me back!
Nor shall I hear your pretty, flattering pleas!
Yet there is one inviolable bond—your lack!

Your need shall draw me from the last remotest star

From an Old London Notebook

That whirls through dizzy space!
And I will come ... as surely as the light!
Without your call, nor yet an urgent sigh!
This is my creed.

I'll come inevitably upon the wing
Of some great eagle ... not a bluebird now!
I will come back for this one thing!
I, who am wayward ... and wandering!
—Jeanie MacPherson

The Chalice
(The Message)

*Dedicated to Walter Lanyon
in deepest gratitude.*

I will answer your need,
But He it will be
Whose words speak through me!
Whose truth brings the healing
Whenever you bleed.
Listen and heed!

I am but clay
In the Potter's pierced hands!
Only the vessel
That His will commands!
So, when you lift up this vessel
To drink,
Pause there ... and think!

I am the chalice, but He is the wine!
I am the green leaf, but He is the vine!
I am the written scroll, He is the Word!
I am the scabbard, but He is the sword!
I am the servant, but He is the Lord!

2 A.M.

> Pause, then, and think,
> As you drink ... as you sup ...
> And when you have finished,
> Relinquish the cup!
>
> It is no matter
> Which cup hold the wine,
> Whether golden and jeweled
> Or simple and plain!
> Nor if it be shattered,
> For He will remain,
>
> ... Forever ...
> The wine and the vine!
> The Word and the sword!
> Our Lord!
>
> —Jeanie MacPherson

Wait

"Wait patiently on him, and he will bring it to pass." Does not say perhaps or maybe. It says He *will* bring it to pass. That is where the teeter-totter goes down on the other side—*your* side, if you can wait—because it is going to happen.

The native Australian throws his boomerang, which describes a circle and falls eventually at his feet. While all illustrations are inadequate to express the wonders of this God-power, yet, in a way, that is what happens to the spoken word. When it is *actually* spoken from the Consciousness instead of from the human thought, it goes out and circumscribes all the manifestation of that human thought and returns to its sender.

From an Old London Notebook

Yet again, it is as if a charged electric wire ran out and encircled all the evil manifestation, and when it came back again to its starting point and short-circuited, burned up all that it had encircled. This may take, to the human sense, some time, but remember that God is *not* (no matter what the human belief says) mocked. It says *is not*—and so wait … wait … wait patiently for Me. *I* am that wonderful Power which is gathering in the whole harvest so that the tares may be burned.

At the very moment that you may be wondering why something doesn't happen to heal the disease, to destroy the enemy, to bring out the harmony—suddenly it comes into being, and the entire manifestation of evil is destroyed, burned to a crisp.

Do you have any idea what happens to a person who touches a high-voltage wire? It doesn't just sear the flesh—it burns it to a crisp. And that is the way this wonderful Truth acts on the evil manifestation that has been cluttering up your life. Wait for Me—give Me a chance—stand just one split-second after you cannot wait any longer. That is the "hour" you failed to wait with Me before. Now wait—*I* will not fail you.

And such wonderful other commands: "Having done all, stand and see (actually) the salvation of the Lord." There isn't anything (not anything) that can withstand this Power. Hang on just a split-second longer than your human mind can stand it, and you've done the trick.

2 A.M.

Let's Have a Little Private Earthquake

"And there was silence in heaven for the space of an hour," and after that, every sort of thing took place—earthquakes, fires, tornadoes, and every other manifestation which is destructive to the material world of human thinking.

If you can, in your meditations, get into the silence "for the space of an hour," you will find the power of God coming through with such force and swiftness that the old human world, which has found you with its Gibraltars of human belief, will experience plenty of earthquakes, plenty of fires, and plenty of tornadoes, if they are necessary to uproot the time-honored and chronic beliefs of the human mind.

Sometimes the cleansing of the Power is spoken of as the wrath of God, but the wrath of God is nothing more than the power of God coming into manifestation. What it does to evil belief may seem wrathful, but that is only because it is being driven out of the temple with its money changers and dove sellers. In that immeasurable space of time, that "hour," a wholly new basis of life is made manifest.

Human laws and thoughts get pretty strong at times. Peter had to have an "earthquake" to show the toughest human law or thought that he was to be released from his prison. When this "silence for the space of an hour" takes place, the jailer will, as he did in the case of Peter, be glad to have you be

From an Old London Notebook

gone from his jail. After all, you cannot run a jail if earthquakes are always going to knock it down.

"His rebuke was terrible" is another way of putting it. Remembering the words of Jesus, one takes courage and eventually finds out the truth of his blessed words. The old human thought may be pretty well-established and entrenched in accepted beliefs, and perhaps it will take an earthquake to jar them loose, but when that happens—and it could happen to you any time you are pure enough in consciousness—then there will be a wailing and gnashing of teeth.

"Wham!" and the door of the prison house of fear, sin, and disease fly open. The Word has been spoken this time. The silence has gathered such a mass of power at one point as to change the stoutest human mind. He is glad to retire, suddenly finding that "he doesn't want to play anymore"—but it's too late; he has already played his last trump, and it wasn't good enough.

Do you believe in the Word as all-powerful? Do you believe that the spoken Word could shatter the toughest human problem with the same ease that Caruso could shatter a hollow-stemmed champagne glass by singing into it the tone to which it vibrated, intensifying the tone to such a point that the glass could not stand it? So is the word of God, when spoken through you, able to shatter the worst picture of disease, and if you could enter into that silence "for the space of one hour in heaven," then even that seemingly impossible picture called death could be shattered and Life immortal stand forth in all Its fairness and glory.

What are we afraid of? "If ye slay me, yet will I say you are God." Can you stand up to that? You've got nothing to lose and everything to gain. "Nothing is impossible to me," said Jesus, when the liaison with God is perfect, and he also said nothing is impossible to *you*.

"Wham!" Let's have a little private earthquake and get rid of some of this old rubbish that has been identifying itself with us so long. "Let's go."

When He Comes

"When he comes whose place it is to rule." I image this forth as the cloud of Light that suddenly surrounds you the moment you enter the consciousness of the Presence. It is the invisible/visible Light which works the while. As you stand in the presence of some evil situation, talking or arguing with it, this all-penetrating Light is at work disintegrating the strongholds and putting life into static situations.

It is wonderful, for nothing seems to be being done, and yet, all of a sudden, everything has changed, and the evil picture fades out. The ugly manifestation has been devitalized—it is nothing but a memory of a memory now—and presently this shall pass. So "having done all, stand and see." *You* have to do all these things, and you will, when you know that "when he comes whose place it is to rule" is a real thing and not a human belief.

Page Junior

Oh, Junior—I just heard a commentator on the radio say that spinach was not all it was cracked up to be and that it wasn't especially good for little boys. Wasn't that what I heard you say too? Well, perhaps Jesus was right—"The wisdom of man is foolishness in the eyes of God." I told you to stay away from that man "whose breath is in his nostrils" if you didn't want to carry around a pack of lies on your back for the rest of your life. All right, Junior, you needn't make it any harder by adding, "I told you so."

A Couple of Good Words

Two good words to remember are: Jehovah-jireh
In plain English: The Lord Will Provide.
The translation says *will*.

The Pattern

"The pattern shown to him on the mount"—the archetype or the created thing—unchanging, made in the image and likeness of God. Returning to this permanent pattern, the delineation of it on matter becomes more and more perfect.

The archetype remains unchanged. Billions of reproductions of it may be made, copies which disintegrate if not held in place by consciousness.

2 A.M.

The archetypal symbol of substance never increases or decreases. If you are conscious of this Prototype, you will never lack, no matter how many reproductions of it pass through your hands.

The alphabet remains intact no matter what use is made of it. From the original n, you can take as many reproductions as you please without depleting the original n. The fashion of the reproduction is up to you. It can be written in millions of different ways, but it does not change the original.

Jesus, knowing this archetypal thing, always returned to that point in consciousness, and the defective or distorted copy was thereby corrected. To contemplate the permanent, unchanging source of life is to correct the distorted pictures of health and disease which are supposed to be copies of it. It is no good making a copy of a copy of a copy—the moment you start this, defects appear.

The reason you are commanded to "judge not from appearances, but judge righteous judgment" is that the righteous judgment is made from the consciousness of the Prototype—the perfect thing. The moment this is recognized, the distorted congested, human thought-pictures dissolve.

Nothing goes anywhere when sickness is apparently cured—the congested thought is "uncongested." The rubber ball pinched out of shape is set free, and it automatically returns to its natural shape. So with any organ of your body held in thought. It is distorted, and the moment you discover the archetypal model, you release the picture in thought, and the organ or condition returns naturally to normal.

If all the money in the entire world were to be destroyed, it would in no way affect the substance or the original Prototype of it. No wonder, then, that Jesus went within, closed the doors—stopped talking and arguing—and contemplated the presence of the archetypal thing created in the beginning and as changeless as God.

Chapter XVII

Taking Thought

We are taught concentration, we are taught relaxation, and we are taught to speak as one having authority; but until we obey the Law which says, "And I say unto you, take no thought for your life, what ye shall eat or what ye shall drink; nor yet for your body, what ye shall put on" and, "Which of you by taking thought can add one cubit to his stature?" we shall ever be fussing about, trying to think ourselves out of difficulties and finding in the last analysis that we have been largely under self-hypnosis.

If the Law states clearly that nothing is to be changed by thinking, then why does man persist in trying to think himself out of difficulties? A survey of the thinking process of making success, happiness, and health shows clearly that there is more failure than success.

No matter what your opinion may be regarding the subject, you never will change anything in Reality by your thought process. If the eternal verities were to be changed by the mere thinking of man, the whole of existence would be at the mercy of man, and chaos would result. The only thing that is changed by thinking is your attitude toward a thing.

Taking Thought

Some people think that meat is harmful to them, others that they cannot do without it. What about this? Is the help or harm in the meat? It does not follow that because you think a certain way that makes it the same for another. Because you think a thing is good does not necessarily make it so. At one time it was thought to be good to force religion on people, obliging them to attend religious services. Today this is changed

Only beliefs can be changed—realities never can. And so man again finds that he is up against a shifting, changing system of thought. He has beseeched, begged, pleaded, and even demanded what he claimed was his divine heritage, without the slightest result. He has lived upon some far, distant demonstration of the Power and has drained it dry of its inspiration, hoping against hope that he might have a return of the Power. He has asked himself and others why it is that he is unable to heal or get healed, and eventually he turns to the plane of ...

Spirit
"I am of too pure eyes to behold iniquity" is the watchword. Man begins to understand that the power of the Christ-Consciousness, which is quicker than the thought, is *awareness* and not *creation*. For the first time, he sees that his eye has been double; that he has been living in a world of good and evil; that he has had to accept evil before he could get rid of it;

2 A.M.

that if he could get rid of it, it of necessity must have been unreal.

He sees that belief is the only thing that can be changed and that the eternal laws of God cannot be broken. If they could, they would be worthless. What man does is to attempt to break them and is himself broken in the attempt. *Awareness* of his God-Self lifts him to a place of recognition. He sees clearly that all evil is ignorance (ignoring God).

Just as a student of music who ignores the principles of harmony will achieve small results and much discord, so his acceptance of evil as something that has to be got rid of is merely his ignorance of the *Something* that must be recognized. In spite of the injunction "take no thought," thousands of people are today fighting a terrific battle with evil, which is more or less real to them by reason of their acceptance of it.

"Come out from among them (your beliefs), and be ye separate." You can believe anything, but that does not make it true. Eventually man will take the path of pure Christ-Truth, as manifested by Jesus, and will learn there is no time which is before the Christ-Consciousness. "Before Abraham was, I am." That is, there is no "before Christ." There is a "before Jesus." "Before Abraham was, I am," but there is a very definite period prior to the Jesus. The "Jesus" comes and goes, but the Christ remains in His changeless state of glory, waiting recognition.

Taking Thought

If Jesus had not recognized his true Self, the Christ, he would have passed away unknown, an obscure carpenter in a small village. He admitted that as Jesus he could do nothing but that with the Christ he could do anything. He made it perfectly clear that what he did *through* the man Jesus is a present possibility with every man, knowing the impersonal Power which was and is impartial and everywhere instantly available.

Man begins to see that he cannot change the eternal facts of Being. Thousands have said, "Lord, Lord," and received nothing; thousands have said, "Peace, peace," and there was no peace—and thousands have said, "Peace, be still," and seen a raging sea of human belief calmed like a millpond at sundown. No authority rests in the plane of the mental, for its basis is constantly changing.

Not so long ago, people believed that every true prayer should be prefaced with endless denials. This being eventually found unproductive of results, the idea was changed to intense and repeated affirmations of the truth. This too is beginning to crumble. Trying to take the kingdom of heaven by violence has not proved successful. Telling the Creator that He is God and the only Creator is no revelation to God and does not make it any more true than repeating a thousand times over that two times two are four makes four any more than it was before. It has always been that and always will; nothing will ever change that, for it is an eternal verity.

2 A.M.

Gradually man begins to see that all his thought processes have come to naught. He has merely built up a universe of beliefs which he finds tumbling about him. In his desperation, he reaches out for the reality of the spiritual plane, the place of changeless Reality, and begins to experience the first real and enduring peace he has ever known--the peace which passeth all understanding. He sees now that the injunction, "I will overturn and overturn, until he comes whose place it is to rule," is made true, and he is happy at last to be rid of the bulky letter of that teaching which was given to the child and kept from the wise and prudent.

Why man has gone so far afield is the amazing thing, when he begins to see the simplicity of life and the beauty and holiness of the true creation. He smiles when he thinks with Shakespeare, "There is nothing either good or bad, but thinking makes it so," and he sees the utter impossibility of such a creation proceeding from God. Imagine a world that is constantly subject to change by taking thought!

Awakening to the glorious possibilities of the sons of God, man is Self-revealed. In a burst of glory, he suddenly sees the portals of heaven (Self-expression) loom white and glistening before him. He begins to experience here and now his heaven.

He calls from the watchtowers of the universe: It is wonderful!

His name, the name of your I AM, is Wonderful, and the government of the life of your Jesus, your human personality, shall be upon His shoulders.

Beloved, rejoice; it is wonderful. All the tiresome job of governing this erratic personality, which you have called by a special name, falls away. You take My yoke upon you and find My burden is light. My burden is merely the bearing of the testimony to the world that the Law of a changeless universe is here and now effective and that the sons of God are not in any way subject to the limitations of the human personality. Man begins to see that true prayer means alignment with that which *is*, and the consciousness of "thine and mine" passes away and the divine "ours" comes into being.

"Heaven and earth are full of thee." Think of it! You are living, moving, and having your being in the pure substance of Spirit. You do not have to think it into manifestation. You have to recognize that Jesus was a truthsayer and not a liar when he said, "The kingdom of heaven is at hand—it is within you."

Believest thou this—you who read this book—or will you drag in your dead fathers and your qualifications and limitations and your special brands of teaching?

When the eye becomes single, the whole body is full of light—full, not nearly full. Full to overflowing because it has lost the shadow of belief which says there is evil in the universe and that thinking can change it into good. When the eye is single, it will

2 A.M.

perceive Reality instead of belief and will thereby see Reality into manifestation everywhere. It is wonderful.

Before you (who read this book), a new door has opened, the door of Christ. "I am the door," and at the same time, "Behold, I stand at the door." When you, through the process of recognition, know that there is such a thing as a perfect universe, created and sustained by God, who found it very good, you will, by opening the door of your human consciousness, find that *I* am there, ready to enter into expression.

The I AM is your individual expression of the universal God. And no sooner is the door opened than you find that the I AM (your own individual point of consciousness) is the door of every wall, to every room (new state of consciousness), to everything that formed a shell about your good and which you termed problem. Behold! Behold! It is *I*— your real Self. Be not afraid.

Quicker than thought is the thinker of the thought; quicker than the twinkling of an eye. Quicker than any human measure is the I AM— knowing everything, needing nothing, awaiting recognition. *I* must increase; the Christ-Consciousness must come more and more into visibility. You (human beliefs) must decrease. The going of the personality, with its petty desire for fame or name or its holier-than-thou, stone-casting propensities, must decrease in order that the Son of God may come to rule in His own universe.

Contemplation of the perfect universe—not the attempt to create it—will cause your human universe to take on new proportions. The borders of your tent will be enlarged; you will launch out into deep waters; you will sing a new song.

To be "absent from the body and present with the Lord" is not an emotional experience but a present possibility. To be present with your true Self is to find yourself in possession of everything that is necessary to sustain the no-problem state of existence. It is wonderful!

Chapter XVIII

The No-Treatment Man

The answer already exists to any and every mathematical equation you can or ever will think of. No matter whether you know it or not, it equals a certain thing before you even put it down on paper. Because you do not know it does not mean anything. Because you do know it does not make it so. It is so already.

A problem exists only so long as the answer is unknown; the moment you have the answer, you have no problem. A question does not exist after you have the answer. It is merely converted into a statement of fact; a worked-out problem is no problem. This checks perfectly with the statement of the Master, "Before you ask, I will answer, and while you are yet speaking, I will give it unto you." The answer to every human problem (belief) exists before you express the belief.

We see the type-man Jesus overshadowed and finally swallowed up by the Christ-Self. Christ never had a problem; he never had to be healed, helped, prospered, or set in His right place. Jesus experienced all these things. You could not heal Christ, but Jesus might be helped or treated. We see the escape from the misery of the Jesus-man made by the recognition of the Christ. The moment he functioned in the Christ-Consciousness, anything and all things were possible to him; but had he dropped down to the human plane of the Jesus, he might have cried, "My God, why hast thou forsaken me?" as recorded.

Jesus came under the law of birth, breeding, training, environment, and all the rest. He had a history of his own and a human destiny, even as you have, which was blotted out or made nil by the understanding of his true Self, which was above help.

We see the Jesus in the process of recognizing his true Self and escaping the limitations of the human. In the press of the crowd, there was little escape for Jesus; but the Christ was able to take Its manifestation through the crowd unnoticed because the Christ in each "has a way that ye know not of" — and that is not the way of thought, "for eyes have not seen, ears have not heard, neither has it entered into the heart of man the things that God has prepared for them that love him."

The Jesus, or what you might term his human personality, could see no way; he could not think his way out or across the lake unless he went through the limitations of the Jesus-consciousness. But turning to the true Self and recognizing Its presence enabled him to work what people called a miracle, which in reality was but the natural and true expression of the God-Self. It is no miracle for the hungry to be fed in the all-substance of God.

2 A.M.

When Jesus said, "Wist ye not that I must be about my Father's business?" he had already made it clear that his Father was within. He might have stated clearly, "Wist ye not that this Jesus must be about the business of the I AM in me?" In other words, it should be about the business of that Power which does not bow down to the laws of the human limitation. This comes by a process of pure recognition, awareness.

Either the Scriptures are true or they are a lie. What will you do with such statements as, "You say there are yet four months, and then cometh the harvest, but I say unto you, Lift up your eyes and look on the fields; for they are white already to harvest." "Thrust in the sickle."

Jesus could not reap where he had not sown any more than you can, but the Christ could thrust in the sickle because He did not in any way function under the frail laws of the human consciousness. Hence, the importance of recognizing the Father within—not pleading with It but merging the human will and thought unto It and acting from the point of awareness. If God cannot do it, neither you nor ten thousand people are going to accomplish it.

It is no longer a question of demonstrating good; it is a question of getting people to recognize that there is God. Most anyone will challenge that statement, but a short conversation with most Truth students will clearly prove that they believe more in the Power as evil than good. Fifteen minutes of

The No-Treatment Man

conversation will reveal evil of every sort as being stronger and more powerful than good. Few there be who salute the Christ in you and speak the word of Reality. They believe emphatically that evil has to be destroyed, and yet we find that there is nothing in the kingdom of God that can be destroyed. We find that in the Book of Life "nothing can be added to or taken from" the Word, remembering that the Word was made flesh.

What, then, is all this adding of evil and disease that has taken place? It is a failure to recognize that there is God. How could there be God and something else, if God is All and in all? What is the evil that we treat but belief in a power opposed to the supreme Power.

A human law is only local. Sin might be said to be somewhat a matter of geography. In order to fulfill a traffic law in one country, you may be deliberately breaking a traffic law of another.

"Ignorance of the law excuses no man" is more true on the divine plane of the no-treatment man than on the human plane. In fact, you have paid every penalty of unhappiness and limitation by reason of the fact that you were ignoring the law of Spirit, which is "of too pure eyes to behold iniquity." On the human plane, you may run your car fifty miles an hour in a ten-mile zone and pay no penalty except you are apprehended, but this is not so in the universe of the All-God.

2 A.M.

Were you to make a questionnaire for yourself and have to answer this question, "Who are you?" what would you answer? Being perfectly honest, you would probably say, "My name is John Smith, thirty; I was born in California; I have thus and so much education, breeding, and family; I am subject to certain financial and physical limitations."

But you have denied everything that is true. You are the Son of the living God. Do you hear? I said *living* God, not a God who has been made alive by your thinking process or because you treat Him into existence or because you affirm that it is so. You are the Son—the point of manifestation where the God-power pours out into expression in a constant and endless stream of power, health, substance, and holiness.

As you contemplate this glorious revelation, you will understand some of the wonderful possibilities that lie just ahead of your John Smith through the door of the I Am Consciousness, which is not created or made to appear by thought but which is recognized as the pure creation of God.

Believest thou this? Do you actually believe that God made the world? If so, what are you going to do about it? If you make your bed in hell, there am *I*. If you ever recognize Me (Father within), in the most hellish situation you can imagine, you will see it instantly fade from the picture and resolve itself into heaven. In other words, you will rend the veil of human belief and find the thing you have been

The No-Treatment Man

seeking standing eternally in its right place and merely waiting the coming of the Master, who will recognize it as true without trying to create it.

Is there actually any truth to the statement that God created the world, found it good, and rested—and that He is a changeless power? Do you believe it? Or would you just like to believe it? Is it so that the kingdom of heaven is at hand? Or is that just a fairy tale? Is it possible to have a host of sick, sinning, and evil things in heaven in order that you may be glorified in treating them out of existence?

"Pray without ceasing" does not mean an endless, monotonous telling God about your troubles and of His qualities, but it does mean a constant capacity to be aware of the only living God as here and now—and rejoicing over the presence of the kingdom here and now.

No wonder that such a magnificent thing is given to the child (the consciousness that can accept God without question) instead of the adult (adulterer), who mixes everything true with his impure human reasoning. It has been said, "The wisdom of man is foolishness in the eyes of God," and inversely, "The wisdom of God is foolishness in the eyes of man." Time without number, we find the wisdom of man failing ignominiously; what he learns one year as the height of erudition may the next year be relegated to the dump-heap of ignorance.

Three thousand years of medicine have not decreased disease, no matter how lofty the aims of

2 A.M.

those noble souls who have given their best, and even their human lives, to make this end attainable. We are beginning to see that what Jesus and the prophets said is more than just a fairy tale. We begin to recognize that he spoke of a truth, for he spoke of Himself. He spoke of the pure wisdom that was revealed by recognition that he was and *is* the Son of the living God. And just as soon as you begin to contemplate that state of things, you will see that what you have been trying to demonstrate for years is actually awaiting your appropriation.

The more we think of evil the more aggravated it becomes, until it increases to a point of self-destruction. Everybody has at one time or another built himself a Goliath and had it threaten his city (state of consciousness) with complete destruction, and at such time he has called for his David with his five spiritual senses and destroyed or wiped out the manifestation of belief.

Eventually you will find that you have eyes and see instead of eyes and see not. In other words, you will perceive what it means to become aware of your true Self. A body that is always in mind is a sick or ailing body; a pocketbook that is always in mind is flat; a state of life that is constantly toyed with in an attempt to make it better will only result in a poorer manifestation. Rather, then, "be absent from the body and present with the Lord" sums up the teaching of recognition. When your thinking process is off evil, evil ceases to function, for it is sustained only by the

The No-Treatment Man

thought process. It has no divine mandate for existence and finds its substance in the ignorance of man, who thinks it is something real that he must call upon God to destroy. Just so long as he does this, he will operate on the mental plane of life and not experience the glorious freedom of the child of the most High.

Job's captivity was changed when he stopped trying to change it. When he prayed for his neighbors, his captivity was turned, and he had twice as much as he had before. It is interesting that this should have happened after his almost ceaseless praying, beseeching, begging God to help him. We see very clearly that it is in taking thought that we produce the evil of life. The John Smith that does not recognize his true Self suffers with Job—he is always trying to save the world or himself instead of standing on the heights of Reality and revealing the kingdom of heaven as here and now. You begin to recognize why it is wonderful.

The no-treatment man is the Son of the living God. He constantly lives in heaven (a state of consciousness), and he speaks of himself. John Smith then takes up the word and goes through the mechanics and says, "I speak not of myself, but him that sent me into expression."

We are at this very point of walking through the door and finding that, like the drop of water, we are one with the sea of substance, the sea of Spirit. As the candle flame is lost in the sunlight yet retains its

2 A.M.

individuality, so the individual loses his sense of separation and limitation and takes on the proportions of his God-given Self. He sees with the eyes of Spirit, which cannot behold evil. Not that he wants to shut his eyes to anything, but he actually sees as Jesus the Christ saw, when he looked through the belief of ignorance that was binding a cripple and said, addressing the Christ in him, "Rise up and walk." The human personality had already testified to the fact that he could not move.

Jesus did not go to Lazarus to make him alive; he went to awaken him, stating that he had fallen asleep. Do you suppose that the restoration of the withered arm was as slow as thought? It came instantly—the physical could not perceive its possibility because it saw through a glass, darkly, and saw the human history as real. Jesus, through his at-one-ment with the Father within, perceived the man whole and perfect, and it was to this that he addressed the command, "Stretch forth thy hand."

"He who hears, obeys," and when you come to understand your true Self, you will appropriate the gifts in a natural, normal way. Just as soon as the self-seeking is gone and you realize the uselessness of self-seeking, you will be the avenue through which pours the endless stream of God-manifestation. To decree is to see it come forth.

The Son of God, the non-treatment man who needs only to be recognized, approximates his spiritual qualities. He has the seeing eye, the hearing ear, and the gift of Self-revelation. Awake thou, Lazarus, bound up in the filthy graveclothes of thine own making, and "rise and shine, for thy light has come."

"Now is the accepted time." "Now are we the Sons of God." Do you hear? A thousand petty despots who have the world to save will pass away —but My word shall not pass away. You are My word made flesh. You, John Smith, are the word of the I AM made flesh—and now we see the possibility of bringing up this garment to a higher and finer state of beauty and power. We begin to see that as we become acquainted with the God-Self, the human garment will take on finer states of health, wealth, and happiness. These will follow naturally. Your contemplation will then be about "whatsoever things are pure, whatsoever things are lovely, whatsoever things are of good report," and you will see these words made flesh, dwelling among you.

Who are you, and to what end were you born? Are you just another bit of humanity, to be tossed about from one fearful experience to another, to go down into the grave of defeat? Or are you the Son of the living God, *here* and *now* present, in full possession of your true capacity? Awake, awake, awake. It is wonderful.

Chapter XIX

The Dimension of Infinity

The Truth as revealed by Jesus Christ—the Word made flesh, the nature of God incarnate, the automatic power of the universe—is a new dimension, the dimension of Infinity, if we could understand such a paradoxical expression. What the fourth dimension is to mathematics, the revelation of Jesus Christ is to the mechanics of the human mind.

Every statement of this new dimension is outside of the laws of matter. It is completely in the realm of the impossible, improbable, and impractical. Viewed through the "glass, darkly" of human intellect, it is almost pure fantasy, or at best, imagination. Handled by the "thought" of man, it is dissected and found to have no life or existence.

The question "who by taking thought ... ?" is an insult to the wisdom of man. His whole wisdom and intellect are gathered by an elaborate thought process, and though it may, for a moment, seem to be anchored to evidence as solid and unshakable as the Rock of Gibraltar, yet at some future date, the impregnable fortress of wisdom is shaken to its base by being approached from a higher level of thought. The ground fortifications, though they be impenetrable

The Dimension of Infinity

from that level, are completely disregarded by the fast-moving planes.

So the best arguments and defenses of the human thought are not considered by this fast-moving "Jesus Christ principle" of which Jesus the carpenter became aware and gave to the universe.

We speak of Jesus Christ not as a man, not as the son of the carpenter, but as a principle embodying all the concepts and eternal ideas of the *whole* universe and being the type, or matrix, of every man.

At the moment of awareness of this Presence (the Word made flesh), Jesus (the symbol) is changed into the incarnate Power. Heaven and earth meet—the Word is made flesh; matter and Spirit mingle in a third substance which we call Jesus Christ. The moment Jesus becomes aware of this Presence, he is no more Jesus the carpenter, but he is *everything*; at the same time, he is *nothing*.

Loosing or letting go of the Jesus, who admitted "I can of myself do nothing," he finds his Life and exclaims, "I can do all things." The narrow confines of the human consciousness can no more hold this Principle than can the four walls of the most glorious cathedral hold God—and yet that is precisely what it does. Man cannot experience It within himself until he can find It everywhere, and then It is *everywhere*, even within himself, and the trying to make it so drops entirely out of the plan of things.

"You shall find your life when you lose it" becomes a glorious letting go of the personal and a

2 A.M.

living in the impersonal, which personalizes itself again, minus all the limitations of the former self.

As electricity remains unknown until it is given a body (it is everywhere, but it is nothing as far as the senses of man are concerned) the moment the contact is made, it becomes *something* definitely pointed into expression; the Word has become flesh, and "all flesh shall see it together."

The man Jesus, discovering this strange and wonderful Principle common to all men, possible to anyone who would recognize Its presence and let go of the narrow limits of the human thinking process, also knew that because of Its simplicity It would be met, measured, and found wanting by the human intellect. Hence, the sweeping statement, "The wisdom of man is foolishness in the eyes of God." The measuring and dissecting of Spirit is foolishness in the eyes of this Power, which works entirely outside of the narrow confines of matter, in order that It may work through this same substance, transmuting it and changing the meal into leaven.

The great failure of the Truth movement is that it is approached through the "thought-taking" method, yet it is definitely stated that nothing can be accomplished by "taking thought." Thoughts emanate from a state of consciousness, and consciousness cannot be changed from without. The moment anything new is perceived, a wholly *new* aura, or plethora, of thoughts starts to emanate through the mists of the former beliefs and finally clears the ground, as it were.

To think a truth may have a certain virtue over evil thinking, but the sum total of the result may be negligible. Thinking over and over a law of mathematics or music does not produce anything in the manifest world. "Go thou and do likewise" is a requisite, no matter what may be said to the contrary.

The beggar at the temple gate would still be there if he had not suddenly (outside of the thought process) made the gesture and *done likewise*. One moment of thought on the command "rise and walk" would have produced what forty years of this thinking had produced: his inability to move from where he lay.

Until one sees that it is impossible to manifest this Power through the channels of the human thought, he will still try to guide, direct, or make the Power work. Until he moves into the *dimension* of the Presence, he cannot see It in the flesh. Jesus constantly asking, "Believest thou this?" is talking outside of the thought process.

What man, blind from birth, can believe from the human standpoint that he can see? What man, crippled from birth, can believe that he can walk? The more he thinks of it the more impossible it becomes. Dissect it, and you find such an elaborate movement necessary as to stun the human thinking.

2 A.M.

Have you ever thought what would have to take place before a man born blind could see? Well, think it over, and then in your imagination try to construct the eye, threading the intricate nerves and muscles into their proper relation with the rest of the body, and then answer this question, "Believest that I am able to do this for thee?"

If "the wisdom of man is foolishness in the eyes of God," then nothing he can offer on the subject of the how, the why, or the when of this invisible Power could possibly have any bearing whatsoever on the subject.

"Leave all, follow me" is a big command. It causes you to "judge not from appearances," but to "judge righteous judgment." To many, this has been a sermon on charity, but it is anything but this. It is moving into this new *dimension* and disregarding the laws of the lower dimension and the results accruing therefrom.

The story of the shadow kingdom, or the realm of the two-dimensional plane, where a chalk line constituted a prison, beautifully illustrates this point. The story continues that a three-dimensional being one day entered this kingdom and found a man in a prison made of a single chalk line circle. Getting into communication with this shadow being, he was finally persuaded to stand up. To his amazement, when he was standing up he no longer knew anything about prison. He could completely disregard the appearances, for in the three-dimensional world, a

The Dimension of Infinity

chalk line does not constitute a prison. No time is spent in overcoming, setting aside, or getting rid of the prison as long as the man is standing up, for he is in the next dimension.

Jesus, coming to a world imprisoned in a network of ugly conscious-thinking, so crystallized and solidified by centuries of beliefs and findings, spent no time in fighting the appearances ("put up your sword"; "ye do not need to fight") because in the dimension of Jesus Christ, that which constituted a prison on the former dimension was nothing but a symbolic chalk line to the present elevation of consciousness.

This chalk line of belief may be anything from an actual prison to an imaginary network of repressions or inhibitions. It might be anything from the most loathsome case of leprosy to the faintest headache—yea, it might be the putrefying flesh soiling its winding-sheet with corruption of death or the dead, futile shroud of life's "te deum." They are all chalk lines to the *new* dimension.

Gradually, man begins to see that at no time was Jesus Christ fighting the so-called problems of the human mind. He did not inquire into the history of the case, was not concerned as to the length of time the chalk line of belief had been there, knowing that to do this was only to intensify the belief. Yet most people of the Truth movement today are busy with the idea that the reason for Jesus' advent in the flesh was to overcome something that was wholly a matter of relativity and which might pass away of its own volition in many instances. He was only concerned with getting the man in the *chalk line prison of belief* to stand up. "If I be lifted up ... ." "Come unto me."

Jacob *struggled* all night with his problem, but in the morning he loosed it and let it go. The man at the temple gate suddenly jumped into the new dimension, so to speak, and found full use of his body in an instant, just as the blind man suddenly opened his eyes and the beliefs of the former dimension were not considered.

"Work out your own (not somebody else's) salvation with fear and trembling." The wonder and the glory of this new dimension, when it begins to even faintly dawn on you, is "fearful" or "awe-ful" in its terrible and wonderful possibilities. The *reverence*, or *fear*, brings with it a sacred recognition of this principle, "which to know aright is life eternal." Even as we faultily know this God do we begin to experience Life, and presently, when we "know aright," it will mean Life eternal, and the casting off and taking on of belief bodies will have given place to the resurrected temple of the risen Lord.

"Arise and shine, for thy light is come, and the glory of the Lord is risen upon thee" takes on a new meaning when you begin to recognize the revelation of Jesus Christ (the divine Nature—your true Nature). You arise in the *new dimension*; you are absent from the body and present with the Power;

The Dimension of Infinity

and suddenly, when you look out again, the place thereof is no more. The former things have passed away—the chalk line is no more a prison, and so the earth is filled with the light of the new revelation.

Fighting with the problem, trying to bring God down to the level of the human consciousness, is impossible. Invitation is constantly given you—"Arise," "Come unto me," "Open your eyes," "Look again"—and all these gestures are made outside of the dimension of conscious thinking. The prodigal, suddenly coming upon this Jesus Christ Nature said, "I will arise and go unto my Father." It is wonderful what can be accomplished in you when you work by the way of Jesus' revelation. "Go thou and do likewise" is not so "in-understandable" when you see the possibilities of your Jesus Christ Nature taking command.

"Let that mind be in you which was also in Christ Jesus." Let the divine Nature come forth, which has "a way ye know not of" and the ways of which are "past finding out." It need only be recognized, "Behold, I stand at the door and knock: if any (that includes you) man hear my voice, and will open unto me, I will come in to him, and sup with him and he with me."

It is wonderful when you begin to see, even faintly, the way of the Jesus Christ Nature—your true Self. It is wonderful to sense the facts of existence outside of the laws of the human consciousness.

2 A.M.

No more does the human thought wear itself out trying to do things which it knows are impossible. In the resurrected state of the Jesus Christ Consciousness, it is not trying to do the impossible. On this level, it is the possible and natural which is eternally taking place. The Jesus Christ Consciousness is not concerned in setting aside human laws. It is concerned with Its own expression of harmony and joy, and this pattern of Infinity coming into being apparently sets aside or destroys the laws of the dimension of human thought. Hence, a man sick, incurable, or dead in one dimension is well and alive in the other, and the prison house of thought caves in or falls apart at the moment of recognition of this Jesus Christ Consciousness.

When Jesus walked upon the water, it was because of the fact that the consciousness of Jesus Christ was not under the law of gravity, cohesion, adhesion, attraction, etc. When Jesus brought forth the bread and fishes, the wine and gold, he was not setting aside a law but showing forth a new dimension, and the moment the Jesus Christ Consciousness comes into the picture, the shadows of the former things give way. They can do nothing else. "I come not to destroy, but to fulfill," but in the fulfilling, the shadow limitations of conscious thinking may be broken to bits.

At the sound of his voice (the voice of this Jesus Christ Nature), the earth melted. Every law of the

The Dimension of Infinity

conscious-thinking was disregarded—the hills danced, and the way became smooth.

When this is faintly conceived, you will understand why we are not concerned with argument on the Truth. The revelation of the Presence is far beyond argument and so sudden in its effects. Arguments belong to the man "whose breath is in his nostrils." He sees two powers and is attempting, no matter how sincerely, to overcome one with the other. He is doomed to failure, for on this plane of duality, evil is stronger than good.

Living under the conscious-thinking, evil comes into manifestation uninvited and apparently unthought of. The best living ones are not immune from the most terrible disease, thieves, and fearsome accidents. There is no insurance against the onslaught of the devil, call him what you will. The adamant walls of Jericho shut him away from his kingdom, and try as he will, he cannot scale them or destroy them, but when he leaves all and follows Me—then the story is different, and these very walls, so terrible and impenetrable, crumble into dust or are blown into oblivion by the voice of Jesus Christ.

Jesus Christ, the Word made flesh, the flesh made Spirit, is the nature of every man, the expression of which brings into view harmony, happiness, substance, and all things that the conscious-thinking has tried to gain "by the sweat of his brow."

2 A.M.

Fear not—"ye shall reap, if ye faint not." The command "thrust in the sickle" is a big order for one who has not even planted, and wavering between the "Yea, yea, Lord" and the avalanche of human thought and the fearful appearances, it is small wonder that the little encouragement and reassurance is given and needed.

"Be of good cheer, I have overcome the world." The Jesus Christ shall "overcome" (come over) the whole belief of the world, which is your own objectified consciousness. As you come to "feel" the naturalness of Life in Jesus Christ, the old habit of fighting against things will give place to the recognition of God as here, there, and everywhere.

Jesus, coming through the streets of a veritable hell of human belief, joyously proclaiming the kingdom of heaven as being at hand, was so misunderstood that they wanted to destroy him for the good of the people at large. Yet did he proclaim it from the heights of the Jesus Christ Nature, at which point it was and is eternally true and present.

To be hidden with Christ in God is to "dwell in the secret place," above the beliefs of human consciousness. Yet with all this glorious ethereal idea, its intense practicality makes it possible to live *in* the world. The world, to the Jesus Christ Nature, is heaven, and if anything in the world touches even the hem of his robe, virtue proceeds out into expression and, to the human sense, healing takes place.

176

"I come not to destroy, but to fulfill." The Jesus Christ Nature in the midst of you comes to reveal the presence of the next dimension, which is out from under the curse of the law of duality. When you begin to see God here, there, and everywhere, your whole body is filled with Light, and everything you look upon is touched with this divine revelation. Even the fields so barren and brown are suddenly white with harvest.

Within the temple of your consciousness, all these lovely rites are performed. Gradually, man goes within to the Father and there finds something which transcends the human thinking and brings him to the point of "behold." When man is beholding, he is praising the Presence and glorifying the Power and giving thanks to the Power, and these offices cause endless manifestation to become visible. "The glory of the Lord fills the house," the consciousness, and it reaches to the uttermost parts of the earth.

The prison of conscious thinking becomes a chalk line which can go or stay as far as its influence on you is concerned. "Be absent from the body and present with the Lord," present with the Jesus Christ Consciousness within you. It is wonderful—and so it is.

Chapter XX

Mary

I have always wondered why there was not a chapter in the Bible about Mary. She was overshadowed by the Spirit to such an extent that all the biological and physiological laws of the human thought were made as naught. Upon her, in many ways, rests the new revelation. She was the first one to literally put on earth that which she conceived in consciousness.

After having the great over-shadowing of Spirit, she went within and "magnified" the power of the Lord. It needed to be magnified in order to bring out "the impossible." No one would believe her because they knew it was impossible, and by the laws of their Fathers it could not happen—but it did.

No one believes you when you tell of the immaculate conception—the borning of the new idea in you. No one believes that you are going to stir from the old futile and monotonous routine of your life. They all know you too well. That is why you must go within and magnify the Power—and tell no man, for there are many things that you must and will perform before the new manifestation shall be placed on earth.

Yes, there is very little we read of Mary in the Bible. One wonders about the things that might have taken place during the monotonous "te deum" of the carpenter shop in a small provincial town, and yet surely things did happen.

At the wedding feast in Cana, out of a clear sky she calls Jesus to her and simply asks him to set aside all laws of chemistry, physics, and human erudition.

> "And when they wanted wine, the mother of Jesus said unto him, They have no wine."

Just like that—they have no wine. She knew the family budget and at least was familiar with the laws of human life sufficiently to know that simply making a statement, "They have no wine," would not accomplish anything but a negative agreement with most human minds. But (and that, incidentally, is why she must have recognized the Power) she called upon our precious One. It must have been with full belief—no argument.

Do you begin to sense the immaculate conception idea? The bringing forth of the impossible? Mary stands for that. And so Jesus did what was necessary because he couldn't do anything else—and neither can you when once you recognize your divinity. That is all.

And then we see Jesus producing the "best" wine. There is nothing niggardly or economizing in the mind of God—that, too, is in the human thought.

2 A.M.

It begins at the best and deteriorates into the worst through the limitations of human thinking.

"Search the scriptures; for in them ye think ye have life eternal"—and ye have, if ye can take it. And please note in John 2, verse 3:

> "And when they wanted wine, the mother of Jesus said unto him, They have no wine."

What I want you to note is the comma, followed by a new sentence. It would seem that one of the established laws of publication is roughly handled. El Greco, the famous Spanish painter, found it necessary to distort his characters in order to convey emotions and unseen states of mind. So likewise, in this new statement of truth, it is necessary to take liberties with grammar and syntax.

In Far Cathay

In far Cathay, a soldier rested for a moment after the harrowing experiences of the tropics and the horror-filled islands—and thus he wrote (Letter No. 1):

> China, May 11, 1944
> 16th Fighter Squadron

Dear W. L.,
> Although I am well aware that countless letters may be coming to you from all parts of the world, I also feel the urge to add my gratitude and appreciation to theirs. The divine Commanding Officer within myself has spoken, and so, to fulfill the law of obedience, this letter.

For two-and-a-half years, I have been a part of this not-too-pleasant drama which the world has come tardily to acclaim the greatest show on earth. Australia, Indies, and now China have been my homes, and while it has given me much experience and divine adjustment, it has definitely proven to be one of the outstanding experiences in my life. What it has done to me I need not mention because I believe that you have seen more of the world than I have, and surely we are not so different that similar unfoldments should not occur.

Throughout my present earth experience, I have been aware of definite periods of great inflow of new inspiration and confirmation. Everything will go along on a certain level, and then, pronto, something comes—a book or a friend or an experience—which is not unlike coming suddenly to the top of a hill with a wondrous and as yet unseen view. The ones that have occurred before this need not be mentioned now, but I did want to let you know about this one and how grateful I am to you for being such a blessed "stepper-downer" of such blessed help.

A copy of *Without the Smell of Fire* was sent to me by my mother, and it is so wonderful—the whole thing from beginning to end is filled with that sense of bursting joy which cannot be described but must be experienced, and it confirmed throughout truths which have been coming to me during these fruitful yet frightful months of discipline. It gave me definite ideas on the "not thinking" and the raising of the entire

2 A.M.

consciousness, and I am going to ponder these things in my heart, for you are aware of the wonders and the vistas which have and are unfolding.

This is one of the most blessed things that has come my way and the most wonderful "goodness" which has come to me in this strange land. It is to me what the "good earth" is to the devotees of the soil.

God is with you, and I am glad. Thank you again and again for being what you are. To change the last sentence of your book a wee bit (the last sentence of the dedication), I say, "Let me be among the first to say to you, the author: I think you're wonderful."

Gratefully and sincerely,
J.

And then after long months (excerpts from Letter No. 2):

At last the wandering boy is home again, and believe me, although I go about as one in a dream, I'm of the most joyous mortals(?) alive. Now that I am here, it seems as though I have never been away, which in a way is a sort of confirmation of the fact that the present is all that is.

Our trip home was not too unpleasant, although I became very tired of looking at the water for so long. You see, we were trying to give Brother Noah a little competition (on the seas for forty days).

On many of those dark days, when dull skies and leaden seas surrounded us in all of its utter desolation and after the long, long waiting, it drove me to the hold—and then the revelation of the Presence and your blessed book served as a window through which I could grasp and view greater things. It stimulated my thinking so thrillingly that no outer grayness could any longer remain gray under the brilliant whiteness of the inner joy, and my world would take on the glories of the new Jerusalem.

. . . .

… A book or a teacher would always make his approach toward me, and the light would be there waiting to be absorbed. I have not *read* your book—I have *pondered* over it, sentence by sentence. The words were often blotted from view, and then there were those that brought entirely new thoughts to mind, and then I would lay the book aside and write a book about that *one* sentence. And then perhaps an even greater thought would unfold, and so on and on for hours, far removed from the salty sea—immersed in the sea of Light and illumination I rested. I read the things you did not set up on paper. It seemed to me that each sentence in the book had a sort of Light-sentence attached to it . . .

And so went the lovely recording of a soul partaking of the real Light. I quoted the portions of this letter I thought would bring illumination to you and not glory to me. Note, therefore, the vibrant phrase, "the divine Commanding Officer within me has spoken." Remember the centurion?—"for I also am a man in authority," etc.

2 A.M.

And then, "Through the fruitful and frightful months of discipline," and again, "It seemed to me each sentence had a Light-sentence behind it."

Isn't that what we discover about the words of Jesus—that the Light-sentence behind his laws gives us the actual food—the bread from heaven?

Akhenaten's Prayer

> I breathe the sweet breath
> Which comes forth from Thy mouth.
> I behold Thy beauty every day.
> It is my desire that I hear Thy sweet voice
> In the north wind,
> That my limbs may be rejuvenated
> With life through love of Thee.
> Give me Thy hands, holding Thy spirit,
> That I may receive it and may live by it.
> Call Thou upon my name unto eternity,
> And it shall never fail.

About the Author

Walter Lanyon was highly respected as a spiritual teacher of Truth. He traveled and lectured to capacity crowds all over the world, basing his lectures, as he said, "solely on the revelation of Jesus Christ."

At one point, he underwent a profound spiritual awakening, in which he felt "plain dumb with the wonder of the revelation." This enlightening experience "was enough to change everything in my life and open the doors of the heaven that Jesus spoke of as here and now.

I know what it was. I lost my personality; it fell off of me like an old rag. It just wasn't the same anymore."

His prolific writings continue to be sought out for their timeless message, put forth in a simple, direct manner, and they have much to offer serious spiritual seekers.

Walter Clemow Lanyon was born in the U.S. on October 27, 1887, and he passed away in California on July 4, 1967.

Printed in Great Britain
by Amazon